INTRODUCTION TO EDUCATIONAL METHOD

INTRODUCTION TO
EDUCATIONAL METHOD

H. M. KNOX
M.A., B.Ed., Ph.D.

Professor of Education
The Queen's University of Belfast

OLDBOURNE
LONDON

OLDBOURNE BOOK CO. LTD.
121 Fleet Street, London, E.C.4.

© *Oldbourne Book Co. Ltd.*, 1961
Reprinted 1963

*Set in face as Imprint and printed in Great Britain
by Jarrold & Sons Ltd., Norwich*

CONTENTS

FOREWORD

THIS book is intended as a textbook for students in training to be teachers. Its purpose is to give a concise account of the idea of method as applied to various aspects of the teacher's work—classroom practice, the curriculum, the use and abuse of aids, constructing examinations, and the formation of character. It deals mainly with general principles and is not meant to cover in detail special teaching techniques. Numerous books on teaching method, dealing with the problem directly, are already available, and the present work is rather more historical and synoptic in approach. It is hoped that intending teachers will find some background knowledge of the growth of method helpful in enabling them to see in better perspective the development of their art. Teachers may be largely born rather than made, but it is possible to increase native potential by the study of educational method. Science is the correlative of art, and if education is hardly a science in itself we may perhaps claim that there is, nevertheless, a science of education. A critical approach to method in education has a valuable contribution to make to educational thinking as well as to the teacher's professional knowledge, and nowadays no one actively engaged in teaching can afford to ignore the findings of educational science. Grateful acknowledgement is made to Dr. R. R. Rusk, formerly director of the Scottish Council for Research in Education, for helpful suggestions.

CHAPTER I

THE NATURE OF TEACHING METHOD

METHOD in education, as elsewhere, represents a co-ordinated system of principles for the conduct of practice, and until this is generally accepted it is vain to expect teaching to rank as more than a purely empirical art. The informal application in the classroom of the same unconscious psychology that determines ordinary social intercourse is scarcely an adequate basis for successful educational practice under modern conditions. Though we may not go so far as to claim, like the American educationist W. H. Kilpatrick, an established philosophy of method, we can at least reasonably hope that a study of some of the more important ideas regarding method in education will contribute to a better understanding of the complex art of teaching. At the outset it is well to distinguish method proper from mere rule of thumb procedure which will at best offer uninspiring guidance to the good intuitive teacher. We may define it as an orderly planned progress towards a given end, implying the conscious application of systematic knowledge to particular teaching situations. Such knowledge we may expect to derive chiefly from observation of the practice of successful educators throughout the centuries, though always with an eye to improving that practice on future occasions. In the teaching process method performs a largely mediative function in reconciling the claims of educational theory with the limitations indicated by educational psychology. We may all agree, for instance, that some knowledge of number is an essential part of everyone's education, but the way we set about teaching arithmetic in any particular case must obviously take into account the kind of pupil we are dealing with. If Tom Jones has a high intelligence quotient we can no doubt adopt a more abstract and theoretical approach; on the other hand, if his intelligence is known to be below average we should clearly be well advised to stick to a concrete and practical syllabus.

One of the reasons why method in teaching has often been viewed with some distrust is that too rigid a distinction has sometimes been drawn between the subject-matter dealt with and the method employed to put it across. Any divorce of this kind is liable to result in the external application of rules of procedure to lesson material that is inherently unsuited to them. The inevitable consequence is to bring the whole idea of method into contempt, and no doubt a main factor in discrediting the well-known Herbartian steps was simply an inveterate tendency on the part of practitioners to apply them indiscriminately to every type of subject-matter. Another cause of difficulty has been lack of precision in defining the exact scope of method in education. Method is often popularly equated with the whole technique of teaching, whereas it is primarily concerned with the most appropriate presentation of lesson material in any given circumstances. It would be unrealistic to attempt to draw any hard and fast line of demarcation, for good method must always constitute an important part of a well-developed teaching technique; but teaching technique is a more comprehensive term embracing the more general requirements of class management, such as the securing of attention, the maintenance of order, and class control. Admittedly, the more successfully method can be adjusted to the needs of the pupils and the requirements of the subject-matter, the less likely are problems of class management to arise. Nevertheless, the terms are not synonymous and certain conceptions of method may even have disruptive effects on what is ordinarily understood by class management. By involving the pupils in movement and conversation the Project Method, for example, may well cut across conventional notions of order and control and yet prove a highly effective way of causing children to learn.

Our interpretation of method must accordingly be sufficiently elastic to embrace methods of learning as well as of teaching, including even deliberate manipulation of the pupil's environment to enable learning to take place incidentally. This is the process underlying the Project Method and it has sometimes been claimed that effective control of the learning situation is ultimately the most efficient method of teaching. To concede this, however, is unduly to restrict the possible range of instruction. Surely the acquiring of skill, training in appreciation, and the fostering of desirable social and religious attitudes in the pupil all demand a more intimate personal relationship between teacher and taught than the mere objective manipulation of environment. It is as well, therefore, to be satisfied with a conception of method which stops short of the status of an established science. Teaching will aways remain a personal art and it may be that method can never develop beyond a set of broad generalizations into an accepted body of systematic doctrine. Nevertheless, the professed aim of much patient educational research is to put method on a scientific footing as compared with the haphazard teaching procedure of the past. The changed attitude to the teaching of Latin is perhaps the most striking example of the gradual recognition of this tendency. For several centuries the masters in English grammar schools devoted their whole energies to the thankless task of attempting to teach a modicum of Latin, from the age of eight, to more or less unselected pupils whose school life might well be relatively brief. Nowadays, however, the Advisory Council for Education in Scotland in its Report on *Secondary Education* (1947) is prepared to recognize explicitly the futility of such unregulated instruction. Instead, they recommend that, however educationally desirable a subject Latin may be, it is likely to prove a profitable study only if taught to pupils whose intelligence quotient is not below 108, for not less than four years from the age of twelve. This represents something approaching a scientific statement of the minimal conditions required for the successful teaching of Latin.

It has not always been fully appreciated that there must be a causal relation between teaching and learning. Teaching methods, however impeccable their outward appearance, will prove valueless unless they are expressly designed to incite in the pupil the activity of learning. Tacit acknowledgement of this fact is to be found in a subtle change of emphasis indicated in the titles of many current works on teaching method. *How to Teach Reading*, or even *The Sentence Method of Teaching Reading*, has been replaced by some such pupil-centred title as *How Children Learn to Read*, *The Improvement of Reading*, or *Learning to Read Through Experience*. The modern conception of method thus tends to represent a continuous search for more economical and efficient ways of enabling the pupil to acquire for himself the requisite experience in the particular field of study. Here, however, we come up against a third problem in our consideration of the nature of method, namely, how far it is possible to ignore the contemporary division of the curriculum into specific branches of knowledge. In other words, is the notion of a general methodology of education any longer tenable, or would it be wiser to abandon the search for general underlying principles and concentrate on the specific procedures applicable to the teaching of individual subjects? So long as the curriculum in the past (i.e. the classics) was closely integrated round the study of language the distinction between general and special method was minimized; but with the growth of interest in the basic skills at the primary stage and the diversification of subjects at the secondary stage the dichotomy has inevitably become more marked in our own day.

It is objected against the idea of general method that each individual subject has its own technique and that, accordingly, the amount of overlap from one to another is questionable. There may be an element of truth in this, though the Project Method, for instance, has to a large extent successfully ignored the existence of separate subjects altogether. Even more conventional methods, such as the Herbartian steps, have succeeded in evolving a technique common to a wide variety of more or less heterogeneous subjects. We are no doubt justified in concluding, therefore, that even if the communal basis of method has been weakened by the increasing fragmentation of knowledge, there are still good grounds for thinking in terms of a general approach to teaching. Nor has special method altogether escaped criticism, as tending to circumscribe the teacher's attitude to his art as a whole. It is unfortunately the case that many specialist teachers do tend to regard themselves merely as experts in English or physics rather than as educators of children through their subjects; but surely the answer to this is simply that courses in special method ought to be so devised as to counteract such an attitude. The study of method should in any case never be so dogmatic as to obtrude on the teacher's natural intercourse with his pupils or to oblige him to be continually adjusting his instruction to its detailed requirements. Fundamentally, methods are very similar for a wide variety of subjects and consequently it is still relevant to promote the study of general method. At the same time we must recognize that since the application of method to each individual subject is not always immediately obvious, there is no inconsistency in advocating in addition the study of special method. To take an analogy from science: nobody disputes the existence of scientific method, yet it would be idle to deny that the physical, biological and social sciences each have an appropriate special method. Similarly in the educational field, the learning process no doubt always offers a certain amount of common ground, though the specific problems of teaching must obviously differ widely from one subject to another. There is, of course, a certain danger of overdoing method, but this can scarcely be regarded as an argument for dispensing with the need for methodology altogether, as some writers would have us believe.

The study of method first began to be recognized as desirable when the teaching of large numbers of children became imperative. The invention of printing and the Protestant doctrine that every man and woman should be in a position to interpret the Scriptures resulted in a much wider diffusion of education. Though the Roman Catholic Church did not accept this view, the Jesuit educators of the sixteenth century were among the earliest to pay attention to the importance of method. They standardized the curriculum in their schools, carefully graded the classes, and drew up model syllabuses in each branch of instruction. It was, however, in the following century that the Moravian educationist, John Amos Comenius (1592–1670), for the first time wrote about method in education in a systematic way. Admittedly, it cannot be said that his approach to the problem was really scientific since in his day the study of psychology was not sufficiently advanced. Relying rather on analogy with natural processes, Comenius contrived to evolve a 'syncretic' method which nevertheless marked an epoch in the development of methodology. His procedure was to take a supposed principle in nature, to illustrate the imitation of this principle in the arts, to indicate deviations from it in classroom practice, and to suggest practical remedies for the resulting situation. The syncretic method in operation thus involved four steps, namely, principle, imitation, deviation, rectification; these Comenius proposed to apply to all three branches of knowledge in the curriculum he prescribed which comprised arts, sciences and languages. It was in languages that Comenius gave most thought to the question of special method. Here he advocated that language teaching should be conducted on recognized principles, that (as he put it) 'matter should precede form', that vocabulary should be selective, and that the material studied should be graduated in difficulty. In practice this meant that he considered the proper order of study should be the mother-tongue, followed by a modern language, before Latin is tackled; and because of what we now call 'retroactive (and proactive) inhibition' (i.e. the tendency for similar disciplines to compete with one another unless one of them is already well established in the mind) he recommended that no two foreign languages should be begun simultaneously. The written and spoken language should come before formal grammar is studied. Not only must individual words be taught in close association with the things they represent but the vocabulary itself should be determined on the basis of a word-frequency count. Finally, the textbooks used should be carefully compiled in a graded series, as we know them today, and not just comprise miscellaneous matter indiscriminately thrown together, as was then the custom. We must acknowledge the essential soundness of Comenius' proposals for language teaching, though we may not think so highly of his more general syncretic method. Nevertheless, even today the usual conception of general method tends to involve the operation of four or five clearly marked steps, however differently conceived these may be from those propounded by Comenius.

The influence of Rousseau served to redirect attention from subject-matter to pupil as the centre of the educative process and towards the end of the eighteenth century the sphere of method was extended to include the early stages of education. The chief contributor to this movement was J. H. Pestalozzi (1746–1827), generally credited with having

originated the object lesson. He attached particular importance to the child's personal experience of things or facts,
to which he applied the term 'Anschauung', and any lesson
which gave the pupil opportunity to see, handle or directly
experience an object was for him an example of this kind
of instruction. It is true, certainly, that in less expert hands
Pestalozzi's approach often degenerated into the disconnected 'object lesson' of Victorian times. His disciple,
Friedrich Froebel (1782–1852), by his systematic arrangement of the 'gifts' and 'occupations' of the Kindergarten,
may be said to have established the notion of method in the
education of the very young on an enduring basis. In his
case also, other practitioners were all too ready to lose sight
of the principle behind his methods and to exaggerate the
outward forms of his apparatus. Another disciple, J. F.
Herbart (1776–1841), while reverting to the traditional preoccupation with the more advanced studies of adolescence,
endeavoured through a properly arranged method of
instruction to find a means of unifying the child's various
interests. Herbart concerned himself with topics as wholes
and in the systematic development of any topic he discerned
four successive stages which he regarded as more or less
generally applicable. In the first, designated 'clearness',
details are presented analytically to enable the pupils to
familiarize themselves with the constituent elements of the
situation. In the second, or 'association', the pupils are
encouraged to suggest informally, by a process of free interrogation, any connections between what they already know
and the new knowledge. At the third stage, called 'system',
these incidental relations are sifted into an organized unity.
Finally, in 'method' the facts and rules learned during the
previous stage are applied and utilized by being put to the
test, often requiring to be amplified at appropriate places
with additional material. In all this Herbart had in mind
mainly the acquisition of knowledge, but once again his
followers hastened to apply his doctrine to every type of

subject-matter, regardless of its suitability for development by this kind of method.

Of Herbert Spencer (1820–1903) it has been said that in formulating the well-known maxims of procedure in his essay on *Intellectual Education* (1854) he was prompted by adherence to the letter rather than the spirit of Pestalozzi's principles. However this may be, these maxims are mainly statements of a traditional kind representing little more than rough and ready guides from which the teacher may select according to the practical needs of the situation. Firstly, Spencer claims, teaching should proceed from the simple to the complex. This is all very well provided the teacher is at pains to determine what is simple and what complex in terms of the pupil's own experience. For Euclid the beautiful simplicity of geometry might proceed from the point to the line, then to the plane figure and finally to the solid; Froebel, however, perceived that the child's actual experience largely reverses this order. If, then, the order seems to run counter to the ordinary development of mental life, we must in our teaching be careful to reconcile the two, although by no means every subject lends itself to development in an orderly way. Secondly, according to Spencer, teaching should proceed from the indefinite to the definite. At first we should be satisfied with approximations, and definition ought to come at the end as a clearing-up process. This is symptomatic of the inductive approach to knowledge, by means of which rules are gradually formulated from preceding examples. Certainly this kind of procedure is obviously appropriate where, as in science, theoretical principles require to be established; where more arbitrary or conventional rules are concerned, as in grammar, its propriety has sometimes been less readily conceded. Nevertheless, if a boy can be got to arrive at Boyle's Law through observing a number of examples, there seems to be no good reason why he should not come to learn the use of the subjunctive in French in much the same way, e.g., by noting that the verb takes a different form after (say) 'je crains que' than it does after 'je crois que'. Thirdly, teaching should proceed from the concrete to the abstract. It is hardly necessary for Spencer to remind us that to begin with things touched and seen before going on to deal with abstractions is a mode of procedure sanctioned by long usage. In the case of young children, particularly, either actual objects or suitably prepared pictorial representations undoubtedly make a most effective contribution to abstract learning. But the maxim should not be uncritically accepted. A lesson may well never rise above the level of the concrete unless the teacher makes a specific point of ensuring its transition to the abstract. Again, subject-matter varies a great deal in the extent to which a clear-cut distinction can be drawn between what is concrete and abstract in relation to it. The term concrete may be taken to cover practical activities as well as technical apparatus, and so no doubt an inherently abstract study like arithmetic can be developed from measuring and weighing to the statement of formal rules. On the other hand, other subjects, or aspects of them, tend by their very nature to be of such an abstract character that even a resourceful teacher has difficulty in finding a concrete starting-point for his lesson.

Fourthly, teaching should proceed from the particular to the general (or, as Spencer puts it, from the empirical to the rational). By this Spencer means that we can expect to establish broad generalizations in the pupil's mind only after laying an adequate basis of factual detail. Again no doubt this is often true enough, although the maxim is beset with pitfalls of a similar kind to the preceding one. The old 'capes and bays' method of geography teaching is a clear instance of a widespread tendency, with factual material, to deal with a mass of particulars which are never generalized. There are, however, subjects such as history which may not really be susceptible of generalization at all except at a fairly advanced level, and in a case of this sort it is plainly futile in the early stages to attempt to pass beyond the particular. Finally, Spencer tells us, teaching should proceed from the known to the unknown. Probably this is the most fundamental of all his maxims, for if the pupil is to take an active share in the educative process his immediate experience must clearly serve as the basis for assimilating fresh material. It is doubtless for this reason that so much importance is nowadays attached in history and geography to local studies and regional surveys. Nobody would claim that of themselves they possess superior intrinsic importance. Their particular value rather resides in the leavening effect which they have in utilizing the pupil's natural environment to extend his knowledge to more remote places and events. In this connection even interest may be almost as valuable as specific knowledge. Boys do not need a profound knowledge of mechanics to appreciate a lesson on the aeroplane or the racing car. Likewise, girls can be told a good deal about the daily life of the Eskimos without necessarily requiring a very thorough grounding in the geography of the Arctic Circle. In general, however, we may agree that the tenor of Spencer's maxims is sound.

Practical guidance of a more precise kind is to be found in the system of Dr. Maria Montessori (1870–1952), who proceeds on the assumption that children's development from infancy to about the age of eleven is best directed by specially graded apparatus rather than left to the discretion of individual teachers. For her the most effective education is self-education, and so the function of the teacher is not so much to instruct in the traditional sense as to supervise the development of the child's psyche. For this purpose Montessori devised appropriate pieces of apparatus to train children in the practical exercises of life such as dressing and hygiene, in the exercises of sensory training such as distinguishing rough from smooth or red from green, and in what she called the 'didactic exercises' of writing, reading and counting. She later went on to discuss methods of dealing with advanced arithmetic, drawing, geometry, music, grammar and verse composition. Depending upon control of the environment, regulation of the child's liberty and the provision of carefully planned material designed to systematize experiences that might otherwise be casual or incidental, Montessori's system has been described as a kind of intellectual discipline by consequences. It takes small account of imaginative training and leaves little room for the teacher's personal influence, though it may claim the merit of re-directing attention to methods of teaching the basic subjects.

The Montessori system is a good example of a 'foolproof' method in which the material presented to the pupil is already properly selected and adapted to his needs in a ready-made theory. The practical effect of such a method is to reduce the teacher's intervention to a minimum and thus to weaken his personal influence as an active participant in the educative process. In these circumstances the training of prospective teachers will be oriented mainly towards knowing when to intervene and when not to intervene in the self-education of the child. To many this may seem an excessive price to pay for dispensing with method of the traditional kind. The danger is probably greatest when excessive reliance is placed on formal apparatus like the gifts of Froebel or the Montessori material, but it is not entirely absent from the educational schemes of the most enlightened exponents of method. It seems clear that Comenius himself was thinking largely in terms of discovering an ideal method which would serve to render individual initiative more or less superfluous and convert the work of teaching into the mechanical task of communicating a predetermined course of instruction. In the United States today great claims are made for automatic teaching by means of teaching machines and programmed learning, and doubtless for routine purposes this technique has something to offer. Happily, it appears unlikely that method will ever be perfected to such a degree as to eliminate the direct influence of the teacher, but we do well to remember that too rigidly prescribed a system may be little better than the complete absence of guidance.

Enlightened method represents a generalization of the intuitive insight or the psychological perception of the great educators of the past. If, therefore, we are to dispense with it in the training of teachers, we must either rely on great natural intuitive insight or else ensure adequate psychological knowledge to improvise teaching technique as occasion demands. No doubt a small number of born teachers do possess the requisite natural insight that makes a formal study of method unnecessary. Doubtless also a sufficiently thorough grounding in psychology will help to illumine the problems of the classroom. The difficulty is that psychology, as now understood, is a complex study which requires a great expenditure of time and labour before it begins to yield practical results. In itself method alone can never be an adequate substitute, and psychology must obviously have its due place in any comprehensive theory of education. Nevertheless, if properly used as an intellectual aid in helping to size up particular teaching situations, a knowledge of method can undoubtedly be of much constructive value to the young teacher. Just as clearly, if this knowledge is allowed to stand in the way of the exercise of common sense, it will prove but a stumbling-block in the beginner's path. Like many other agents, method is a good servant but a bad master.

Suggestions for Further Reading:

Boyd, W., *The History of Western Education*, Black, 1921.
Laurie, S. S., *The Training of Teachers and Methods of Instruction*, C.U.P., 1901.
Panton, J. H., *Modern Teaching Practice and Technique*, Longmans, 1947.
Pinsent, A., *The Principles of Teaching-Method*, Harrap, 1941.
Rusk, R. R., *The Doctrines of the Great Educators*, Macmillan, 1954.
Spencer, H., *On Education*, Williams & Norgate, 1861.
Ward, H., and Roscoe, F., *The Approach to Teaching*, Bell, 1928.

CHAPTER II

THE INDUCTIVE *versus* THE DEDUCTIVE APPROACH

In the presentation of subject-matter to pupils the late Dr. M. W. Keatinge distinguished three broad approaches, which he designated demonstration, heurism and suggestion. The first consisted in simply showing or telling, the second had in view encouraging children to find out for themselves, and the last involved implanting ideas in receptive young minds and allowing them to develop there by a process of germination. Suggestion is, however, rather more restricted in its range of application, and the problem with which the teacher is generally faced is that of deciding whether his function should primarily be to pass on already established knowledge or to train his pupils to discover knowledge by their own initiative. It is difficult to lay down a hard-and-fast rule about this, but the side to which the individual teacher leans must necessarily influence him in his choice of method. The teacher who believes in simply transmitting knowledge will no doubt tend to assume principles as established for the explanation of individual examples. This is known as the 'deductive' method and, on the whole, the majority of classroom situations seem to fit into this pattern. Euclidian geometry is often given as the best example of deductive reasoning, in which necessary conclusions are arrived at from initial premises. On the other hand, as we have seen, while such a method may accord well with the particular kind of subject-matter, it does not correspond with the pupil's natural experience of spatial relations. Accordingly, the teacher who attempts to foster in his pupils a more imaginative and speculative approach to knowledge will rather utilize the individual examples to bring out the general principles underlying them. If this is a more difficult, it is also a more enterprising way of tackling problems of learning, and 'inductive' reasoning of this kind is fortunately commoner in classroom practice than is sometimes supposed. In this case, the data merely suggest, without definitely implying, the generalizations eventually reached. Most scientific discoveries, and creative processes in general, are the result of inductive rather than deductive reasoning.

In this connection John Dewey distinguished between the 'logical' and the 'psychological' order of presentation, his criterion being whether the teacher gives priority of consideration to the matter to be learned or to the needs of the learner. Where these approximately coincide, no problem need exist and the teacher is free to concentrate his attention on a single objective without detriment to either subject-matter or pupil. A sixth-form chemist, eager to gain a reading knowledge of German to further his scientific studies, is a case in point. Unfortunately, however, we cannot regard this state of affairs as typical of normal classroom conditions. Here the teacher generally owes a double allegiance, for, as Sir John Adams long ago pointed out, verbs of teaching (as in Latin) govern two accusatives, one of the person and another of the thing. In order to succeed in teaching John Latin, the master must, therefore, know something both of John and of Latin. This may mean that in practice he is forced to strike a happy balance between the logical and the psychological according to his purpose at a given moment. The pupil's point of view will usually be relatively uncomplicated, namely the most straightforward way of utilizing the subject-matter to achieve the desired result, e.g., get his sum right. The teacher, on the other hand, is likely to be concerned with inculcating abstract principles as well as showing the pupils how to work out a new kind of problem. In order to do so, he may have to sacrifice the psychological order to some extent to the logical, however sympathetic he may be to the needs of his pupils. To be effective his teaching must, nevertheless, succeed in relating the one aspect to the other. The distinction is mainly one of emphasis: broadly speaking, in the early years the teacher does well to concentrate on the psychological needs of the child whereas at a later stage he may increasingly transfer his attention to the logical content of the subject-matter.

In general, the logical order of presentation implies that the subject-matter has been organized in the most systematic possible way. As a rule we may expect to find this kind of treatment in textbooks intended for advanced students, although even then some concession to the psychological standpoint is often made. At this level, as we have seen, the logical order tends to approximate closely to the psychological, but it is unusual for all but the most advanced textbooks to follow a strictly logical arrangement. There may well be an account of the historical development of the particular topic or some other gilding of the pill. Consequently, it is difficult to maintain a clear-cut distinction between logical and psychological in regard to content. From the other standpoint, all that is implied by the psychological order of presentation is that in the selection and arrangement of the subject-matter some consideration be given to the mental experience and intellectual maturity of the pupil. If he is to apprehend the material otherwise than by mere passive reception, it must obviously come within his particular mental grasp. This will necessarily involve on the teacher's part thought and reasoning about the kind of material that is suitable for presentation in such circumstances. But, although the appropriate frame of reference may be simple, the teacher's thought and reasoning will still be essentially logical in character. We can expect, for instance, a normal child of seven to have difficulty in learning to spell a word of more than six letters. The psychological approach may suggest simplification of the usual spelling of longer words, but we may rather try the expedient of presenting to the pupil the letters grouped in syllables with which he is already familiar. Here again we cannot really insist on too rigid a demarcation between the logical and the psychological. In practice what normally happens is that the teacher starts from the logical standpoint of content and approximates so far as need be to the psychological needs of the learner.

Nowadays classroom methods are usually compounded of a judicious mixture of deduction and induction. For centuries the foremost exponent of deduction was the influential Greek thinker, Aristotle (384–322 B.C.). So great was his authority that long after induction had come to be accepted, as a consequence of the teaching of Francis Bacon (1561–1626), as the ordinary basis of the physical sciences, deductive methods continued to dominate the more traditional branches of study. It is hardly surprising, therefore, that the deductive approach was regarded as the natural mode of procedure in teaching, until it reached its culmination in Herbart's doctrine of instruction. The most complete exposition of this educational doctrine is to be found in the well-known five formal steps which were evolved by his followers from Herbart's original stages. The whole method was based on Herbart's theory of 'apperception', a term used to designate the mental process by means of which any new experience tends to be not only interpreted in terms of former experiences but even to some extent determined by the content of what is already in the mind. From this point of view much of the effectiveness of learning will depend on the context in which the material is presented rather than on the illumination of the teaching or the impressionability of the pupil. In Herbart's terminology it is vital that the appropriate 'apperception mass' should be dominant at the time of presentation, and to ensure this more effectively his followers divided Herbart's first stage into its analytic and synthetic aspects. These they called 'preparation' and 'presentation' and they also renamed the last two 'generalization' and 'application', as well as introducing other slight modifications.

The Herbartian system, thus modified, is therefore not purely deductive in character. As its name suggests, the intention of the preparation stage is to prepare the pupil's mind to receive the new material by bringing the relevant apperception mass (or old system of ideas) to the threshold of consciousness. This is done by utilizing systematic questioning on previous lessons in the particular field of study, or on appropriate personal experience of the pupils, to resuscitate in their minds ideas, rules, principles and examples with a view to concentrating attention before actual teaching begins. In the original Herbartian scheme this had to some extent been the purpose of the second stage ('association'), and it is certainly true that much valuable time may be wasted in endeavouring to elicit relevant information from the pupils by way of introduction to a new topic. No doubt they should always be made aware of the purport of the lesson and generally a few brief questions will be the best means of effecting this. But if the topic is entirely fresh or rather outside the usual experience of the pupils, a bald announcement may be all that is required. In a geography lesson on a remote South American republic, it is unlikely that extensive questioning will prove a very profitable introduction unless it should turn out that one of the pupils has a father or an uncle who has been there with the Merchant Navy.

Once again the purpose of the presentation stage is self-explanatory, namely to present the new material itself. Here, however, the teacher adopts a synthetic procedure by grouping together in a logical whole as much fresh subject-matter as can reasonably be absorbed in the time available. Teachers are, unfortunately, prone to overestimate their pupils' assimilative capacity, and the temptation to over-load the presentation stage constitutes a grave weakness in the method as a whole. At the association stage the teacher endeavours by illustration or comparison to link up this new material with the system of familiar ideas which he has already raised in the pupil's mind. If, for instance, he has introduced Archimedes' principle through the ordinary experiences of what happens in a bath, he will now try to relate this information more scientifically with the pupils' previous knowledge about the pressure of fluids. The object of the generalization stage is to summarize and re-present to the pupil the most important aspects of the new material in such a way as to effect, if possible, a modification of his existing mental equipment, or to make explicit for future learning and action the general implications of the lesson. Finally, in application the teacher encourages the pupil to put the newly acquired knowledge to use by reference to fresh examples. In effect, this is chiefly a process of verifi-cation in which the pupil learns to apply what has been learned to concrete cases.

It is easy to pour scorn on the Herbartian steps as utterly outmoded in the modern classroom. They do, however, have the merit of making the teacher think constructively about his lesson material, e.g., how much the pupils know already, how the topic can be most effectively introduced, whether there is a general principle to be extracted, how such a principle may best be applied by the pupils, etc. Again they are useful in planning the distribution of topics in a larger theme, provided the teacher realizes that rigid conformity with the original pattern is not always possible. Presentation must not be taken to imply that the pupils must never be permitted to find out for themselves. Generalization does not necessarily mean that principles are always implicit in the lesson material. Nor can application invariably be allowed to wait till the whole sequence is completed: it must often, on the contrary, be introduced as occasion offers in the development of the subject-matter. Where the Herbartian steps have clearly been abused is indiscriminate application of them to individual lessons in every type of subject. In fact they were never designed for compression of this kind but were intended to be applied to whole topics or 'method units'. Single lessons, as we know them today, are largely the device of time-table makers and, properly regarded, they should be contributory units in some larger whole, e.g. the Industrial Revolution as an integral topic. When correctly interpreted, the Herbartian steps are certainly applicable to a wide variety of teaching situations, but they have undoubted disadvantages. The severely logical approach to learning is unlikely to suit the limited capacity of the average child. The method is also liable to encourage excessive subject-mindedness on the part of the pupil. While it may succeed in developing in his mind a reasonably well integrated system of ideas in mathematics, this can remain in isolation without much overlap with other branches of knowledge. The Herbartians were not unaware of this defect, and as an antidote they prescribed the two devices known as 'correlation' and 'concentration' of studies. These will be discussed later, but in any case their effectiveness in counteracting compartmentalization is open to question. The Herbartian system is essentially a teacher's method and it aims at telling rather than encouraging the pupil to find out for himself. Its object is to introduce the pupil more or less forcibly to a given amount of prescribed material. It may often do so in the way best calculated to make him apprehend and even assimilate it, but by endeavouring to anticipate new situations by which he is likely to be confronted it has for him a future rather than a present reference.

The genuinely inductive method appears to be a relatively modern development, largely due to the emergence of the scientific outlook. Nevertheless, a primitive form of induction seems to have had its advocate in the ancient world in the person of Socrates (469–399 B.C.), who tried by means of a series of simple questions to induce his listeners to discover their own ignorance and need of knowledge. The Socratic method was a process of definition under criticism, in which the teacher invited his hearers to define the nature of certain moral qualities which occurred in the course of discussion. After receiving an approximation to the meaning, Socrates would advance cases not covered by the particular definition offered and this would then be modified until a comprehensive definition was arrived at. The procedure was, therefore, to pass from assumed knowledge, through a state of doubt, to true knowledge which would stand up to rational argument. In simple terms, we begin with a generalization from the facts of ordinary experience and proceed to discover a more rigorous definition of underlying ideas or principles. The phenomenon of combustion, for instance, was popularly accounted for by the presence of an imaginary element, phlogiston, in every combustible body until more rigorous investigation revealed the true explanation in the presence of oxygen in the atmosphere. Though not purely inductive, the Socratic method was clearly inductive in intention.

The present-day teacher does not, like Socrates, seek to elicit from his pupils watertight definitions, but contents himself with the less ambitious task of leading them to a more exact knowledge of his topic. Socrates was dealing with relatively mature young men who had some experience of life and at times he was inclined to break off the argument before reaching the final stage. This technique may serve to stimulate thinking in intelligent adolescents, but it is inadvisable to leave younger children at the end of a lesson in a state of doubt. Nevertheless, although Socrates personally was specially concerned with ethical questions, his method may still, within limits, be relevant to everyday school subjects. Because of its introspective tendency, however, it cannot readily be used for enlarging the pupils' experience of external matters and it can easily degenerate into mere verbalism. On this account, though the Socratic method was approved by Kant, it was condemned by Pestalozzi as unsuitable for teachers and children in ordinary schools. Certainly the Socratic lesson demands from the teacher practised skill in the art of questioning and, in addition, the modern Socrates must, like his great predecessor, be prepared to follow the argument wherever it may chance to lead. Furthermore, the true Socratic lesson should embody an element of paradox. Though it would be presumptuous, therefore, to dub any lesson carried on by question and answer Socratic, Socrates was probably the first educationist fully to appreciate the vital role played by interrogation both in teaching itself and in assessing its results.

Socrates himself used questions mainly for initiating a line of argument or elucidating a principle, but for practical purposes we may nowadays draw a rough distinction between 'teaching' questions and 'testing' questions. The first are primarily intended to stimulate inquiry in the pupils themselves, the second to discover the accuracy of their knowledge of work done. 'Teaching' questions perhaps illustrate best the inductive approach to learning and they also contain a suggestive element which will be considered later; but it is a mistake to make the distinction too sharp. Ultimately all questions, 'testing' as well as 'teaching', are designed to further the purposes of effective learning, and so no teacher may be regarded as competent until he has acquired some skill in the art of interrogation. 'Testing' questions proper can be both oral and written, though oral questioning is more directly concerned with ordinary classroom practice. Indeed, the popularity in everyday life of quizzes, Gallup polls and market research testifies to the value of such interrogation in many other fields. Consideration of written examinations will, therefore, be left till later, but systematic examining of some kind must be deemed an essential part of all successful teaching method.

To be fully effective, oral questions must be purposive in aim, easily comprehensible in form and well within the pupils' normal experience in content. The questioning should be coherent and systematic without switching unexpectedly from one line to another. The language employed ought to be simple, direct, free from ambiguity, and the subject-matter carefully adapted to the pupils' age and stage of development. Well-conducted questioning enlists the co-operation of the class, but a brisk flow of mental energy will be sustained only if the questions asked are not too vague or general. The experienced teacher ought rarely to have to paraphrase his questions, although he may sometimes, like Socrates, require to make his pupils expand their answers. As a rule his questions should be suggestive of a reasonable answer, and, so long as he is fully aware of his purpose, he may sometimes even intentionally so frame them as to define the kind of answer he expects to receive. Unless he particularly wishes to emphasize a point, he should not require to repeat a pupil's answer; and if the answer is wrong it is often best ignored. At all events it is generally wise to avoid drawing attention to error, although when an honest mistake is clearly made the teacher's response should be sympathetic. Even where incorrect answers are suspected of being due to carelessness or deliberate perversity, it is as well to give the benefit of the doubt.

In order to maintain a friendly interchange with the pupils the teacher must address his questions to individuals, distributing them as widely as possible throughout the class. He should be on his guard against employing any form of question which is generally regarded as unsuitable for use in the classroom. The 'rhetorical' question, asked merely for effect, does not really expect an answer, e.g., 'who can deny Shakespeare's greatness?' The so-called 'elliptical' question, usually in the form of an incipient statement broken off in the middle for completion by the pupils, may sometimes not be properly understood, e.g. 'politics is?' (the art of the possible), or 'genius is?' (an infinite capacity for taking pains). More common is the simple alternative or the loosely worded question. Merely to require 'yes' or 'no' for an answer is little better than random guessing. To ask 'does anyone know?' is to encourage chorus answering or, by an implied query such as 'Who can tell me what Boyle's Law states?', to invite an irrelevant response, e.g., 'Boyle'. Another problem in questioning is how far it is appropriate to introduce technical terms. As a general rule, technical vocabulary should not be used until the pupils are reasonably advanced in the subject, but it is possible to carry caution too far. The simpler terms special to geography, even key words in science (like cylinder or condenser) which are also found in everyday life, and certainly the common terminology of ordinary English grammar can be introduced from an early stage as they occur in the subject-matter. It is futile to try to dispense with doublets, such as 'noun' and 'name' or 'time' and 'tense', in the hope of making grammar appear less difficult. The handling of faulty answers calls for the exercise of tact and skill. Inaccurate or incomplete answers can often be unobtrusively amplified by the teacher on the spot, and real misconceptions must clearly be corrected in due course. It is generally the careless or random answer that is best disregarded, since the danger of stamping in mistakes by too much emphasis is never absent.

The teacher who confuses 'testing' with 'teaching' questions may fondly imagine that by merely recalling information he is developing logical thought. It is by no means uncommon to try to pass off the indiscriminate use of questioning as incisive teaching. Really searching questions should challenge the pupils' ingenuity and poor answering may even be a warning to the perceptive teacher that the lesson is not proceeding along the right lines. Nor should the teacher have any monopoly of questioning. In a properly conducted lesson the pupils too should have their opportunity. This has its value for the teacher also in that it gives him an insight into the lucidity of his exposition and the general effectiveness of his approach to the topic. There will, of course, be difficulty in learning to cope with pupils' questions. Too free a flow may well overwhelm the teacher or impede the progress of the lesson. Hence the natural curiosity or impetuousness of the pupils must not be allowed to get out of hand. For this reason, though spontaneity may be inhibited, the inexperienced teacher is probably well advised to make them save up their questions to be dealt with at a particular point in the lesson. A drawback inherent in purely oral questioning is that although answers may be invited from several pupils, the one first accepted tends to steal the thunder. This may rather discourage the others, and the best means of dealing with the situation is sometimes to require short written answers to questions presented orally. Much, however, will depend upon the give-and-take of the moment.

Perhaps the most valuable lesson to be learned from the Socratic method is the important place in all good teaching for effective oral work. Nowhere is this more true than in the teaching of modern languages. Here the so-called 'direct' method is an example of the application of induction in the field of special method. The traditional approach to the teaching of the classics had been largely deductive in nature, although even there occasional attempts had been made to evolve some approximation to the modern direct method. The syntactical complexity of Latin and Greek, together with the difficulty of achieving oral fluency in dead languages, had, however, militated against the success of these experiments. With modern languages it was a different story, yet so strong was the prevailing linguistic tradition that every effort was at first made to make them conform to the old methods. The folly of this was made apparent in

1882 in a well-known pamphlet by Wilhelm Viëtor, entitled *Language Teaching Must be Inverted*. In it Viëtor urged the abandonment of the traditional grind and advocated instead such novelties as oral work, an inductive approach to the teaching of grammar, and the use of interesting reading-matter which included simple rhymes, riddles and stories. Out of this there grew up the direct method in which so far as possible modern foreign languages were taught without the conscious intervention of the vernacular.

Since the direct method is largely the product of a movement, it has never developed a rigid orthodoxy. Broadly speaking, however, it embraces six main principles, though these do not necessarily all have special pedagogic significance. As a starting-point, the spoken language of ordinary conversation is preferred to the slightly obsolescent language of literature. To avoid irrelevant associations with the vernacular, the use of traditional spelling is temporarily abandoned in favour of the international phonetic script. A fluent command of common phrases and idioms is imparted through reading connected texts, dialogues, descriptions and narratives of an interesting kind. In the first instance grammar is taught inductively by grouping together and drawing conclusions from examples noted in the reading-matter, although it is conceded that more systematic study may be required later on. Every effort is made to connect new words as they are encountered, either directly with the objects or ideas represented or with other words in the foreign language that are already familiar—*not* with those of the mother tongue—and to this end object lessons, pictures and oral explanations will largely supersede traditional translation. Written work is not introduced until a fairly late stage and follows a well-defined sequence: first thoroughly explained material is introduced, then stories related orally by the teacher, next free composition by the pupils, and finally exact translation from and into the foreign language.

The aim of induction is observation and imitation rather than exact construction and proof. This may result in some looseness and even inaccuracy, and we must be prepared to accept this penalty if we wish to avoid dullness. At least we do not then put a premium on mistakes of a formal kind, e.g., split infinitives, or the objective case after the verb 'to be', or 'who' instead of 'whom', etc. Logic and grammar are all very well in their place, but excessive emphasis on them in the classroom has a devitalizing effect on the quality of the teaching. The great difficulty with all deductive methods is for the teacher to devise situations in which he can genuinely think along with the pupils. In mathematics this is particularly acute, for here the teacher is constantly posing problems whose answers he already knows or can arrive at in a purely mechanical way. The consequence is that in his teaching he may be tempted to attach more significance to a correct answer than to the processes by which his pupils make the proper inferences. The study of language is perhaps inherently less subject to this particular abuse, but even here deductive methods may easily encourage the teacher to think in terms of how many sentences his pupils can get right in a given time. The advantage of inductive methods, on the other hand, is that they stimulate him rather to bring his pupils to see why they get things wrong.

Suggestions for Further Reading:

Austin, F. M., *The Art of Questioning in the Classroom*, U.L.P., 1949.

Barnard, H. C., *An Introduction to Teaching*, U.L.P., 1952.

Boyd, W., *The History of Western Education*, Black, 1921.

Robson, E. H. A., *How Shall We Train the Teacher of Modern Languages?* Heffer, 1929.

Rusk, R. R., *An Outline of Experimental Education*, Macmillan, 1960.

Smith, F., and Harrison, A. S., *Principles of Class Teaching*, Macmillan, 1937.

Thut, I. N., *The Story of Education*, McGraw-Hill, 1957.

CHAPTER III

THE HEURISTIC PRINCIPLE

WE have it on the authority of A. N. Whitehead that deduction is the primary method of mathematics. With equal justice we may claim that induction is the primary method of science. In connection with his teaching maxims Herbert Spencer says: 'Children should be led to make their own investigations, and to draw their own inferences. They should be *told* as little as possible, and induced to *discover* as much as possible.' This view was evidently shared by H. E. Armstrong (1848–1937), professor of chemistry at the City and Guilds of London Institute, who in 1898 published a celebrated paper, entitled *The Heuristic Method of Teaching, or the Art of Making Children Discover Things for Themselves*. The term is derived from the same Greek verb as 'eureka', more properly 'heureka' (I have discovered it), the cry uttered by Archimedes as he ran from his bath after hitting upon a method of detecting the adulteration of the gold in Hiero's crown. The essence of the heuristic method was, therefore, to set the pupil to find out things for himself, although neither the idea nor, indeed, the term originated with Armstrong. Already in *The Advancement of Learning* (1605) Bacon declares that the man who begins with certainties shall end in doubts, whereas he who is content to begin with doubts shall end in certainties, and in a more specifically educational context something closely akin to the heuristic principle is more than once advocated by Rousseau in *Emile*.

The term 'heuristic' was current in philosophic circles in the middle of last century, and an incidental use of the word in an educational connection has been traced to *The Teacher's Manual of Method* (1858) by William Ross. Armstrong, however, derived his inspiration from a paper read at an international conference on education, held in connection with the Health Exhibition at South Kensington in 1884, by J. M. D. Meiklejohn, professor of education at St. Andrews University. The main theme of this address was a plea for a unified method in educational practice, to be arrived at, Meiklejohn urged, by a scientific survey of the whole field. The amateur plans from time to time produced for the teaching of this or that special subject were, he claimed, as far removed from the methods derived from an objective survey as the rough charts of tramps from ordnance maps. The permanent and universal condition of all method in education was, in his view, that it be heuristic. Originally, therefore, heurism was not conceived as applying to science alone and, indeed, Meiklejohn professed readiness to show that it was also applicable, though in a less degree, to literature.

The heuristic method [he asserted] is the *only* method to be applied in the pure sciences; it is the *best* method in the teaching of the applied sciences; and it is *a* method in the study of those great works of art in language by the greatest minds which go by the general name of literature.

Meiklejohn thus distinguished between method proper and what he called plan, the kind of improvisation forced on the teacher by large classes and external examinations. These gave rise to certain distempers of learning which the heuristic method was designed to counteract. First there was the unco-ordinated miscellaneous information, which Meiklejohn deprecated as encyclopaedism. Then there was second-hand knowledge, which he likened to a kind of fungus betokening the lack of real intellectual life. Next there was the tyranny of books, which precluded contact of one living mind with another. There was also premature instruction, which tended to force on children thoughts and knowledge that at the right age they would gladly welcome for themselves. Finally, there was the temptation to do everything for the pupil by telling instead of teaching, which Meiklejohn called didacticism. 'The pious Pestalozzi', Meiklejohn tells us, 'is filled with measureless remorse when he finds that he has *given* a little boy a conception, instead of inducing him to find it himself.' Nowadays teachers are less didactic and their teaching is less bookish, and we have certainly learned to attach importance to the concept of 'readiness' in pupils before introducing a fresh skill (e.g., tackling reading). Nevertheless, even in our own time Whitehead has found it necessary to pour scorn on the uselessness of mere scraps of information and to protest strongly against the inculcation of inert ideas.

The heuristic movement was always specially oriented towards science. Even before Armstrong, another educational writer, S. S. Laurie, wrote in 1892: 'All science teaching which is not a series of experiments and essentially heuristic is simply word-teaching and charlatanism.' Unless a so-called scientific cause had been experimentally ascertained, it would have no more significance for a schoolboy than a Greek verb. As a chemist, Armstrong was naturally particularly concerned with the specific application of heurism to the teaching of science. Heuristic methods of teaching he defined as 'methods which involve our placing students as far as possible in the attitude of the discoverer—methods which involve their *finding out*, instead of being merely told about things'. Discovery and invention need not be confined to explorers and holders of patents, but could be shared by everyone. The value of mere knowledge had been greatly overrated and too little consideration had been given to the question of how action might be developed by teaching. Armstrong believed, on the contrary, that a teacher's whole duty was to train his pupils to *do*, and he felt that properly conducted experimental work, by its intimate connection with daily practice, afforded a superior means of developing character than other school subjects. The advantages he claimed for the heuristic method were that it fostered interest in common objects and phenomena, it encouraged exactness in measuring not only things but also words and deeds, it formed habits of observing and attending to details, it developed the power of reasoning from observation, and it cultivated manual dexterity.

It would be ingenuous to suppose that Armstrong merely intended that pupils should be allowed to conduct their own experiments in science. What he had in mind was no less than a radical reorganization of school work in general. His method was to involve the abandonment of a good deal of the traditional desk-work and enforced silence of class teaching in favour of group work and mutual discussion. He did not much like the term laboratory, preferring 'workshop'; but though he advocated free activity in place of didactic class teaching, excessive reliance on books and disregard of all tools other than the pen, he had no intention that his workshop method of instruction should overlook practice in the basic skills. Indeed, he claimed that it would cater for this more effectively than traditional methods, which by dictating notes ruined handwriting and through over-emphasis on grammar and composition neglected constructive writing. As an alternative Armstrong proposed that the pupil should keep a daily record of work as the work proceeded, and that this record should be made the basis for a variety of educational exercises. He envisaged, for instance, illustrative drawings by the pupil, correction of spelling mistakes by reference to the dictionary, even use of the subject-matter for linguistic work or translation into a foreign language. The important thing was that the account itself should be so expressed as to make it a personal record of something seen or done by the writer. In this way Armstrong hoped that heurism in science teaching would gradually permeate the whole curriculum and extend to art, literacy, languages and expression. Another important point that Armstrong made was that too ready provision of technical apparatus was apt to throw away valuable opportunities for training. He urged, therefore, that in the workshop every effort should be made to construct any necessary appliances from ordinary articles, such as medicine bottles or jam-jars. He did concede, however, the necessity of exact measuring instruments, particularly a balance for weighing.

Such, then, was the heuristic method as propounded by Armstrong. Like that of Socrates, its aim is to discover, though in this instance the truths of science rather than the principles of morality. The more enthusiastic advocates of heurism attached considerable importance to the requirement that the pupil's attitude should be that of the original discoverer of knowledge. They tried to insist that the procedure to be followed in acquiring knowledge must recapitulate or epitomize the stages through which humanity had passed in attaining it. This presented obvious difficulties, yet heurism was soon enthusiastically adopted in a large number of schools in preference to the traditional 'didactic' type of teaching. As Armstrong hoped, attempts were made to apply it to other subjects in the curriculum. In 1907 Sir Philip Hartog suggested in *The Writing of English* that since really original work in physics and chemistry could hardly be expected from adolescents, the mother tongue might actually offer a more fruitful field for a heuristic approach to the methods of scientific inquiry and research. No doubt the vernacular has potentialities as a readily accessible medium for experimentation, though few would be disposed to treat this curious proposal as other than something of a *tour de force*. Still, it does draw attention to a fundamental problem: namely, that whatever attitude the pupil may adopt towards his work, he can never really hope to put himself exactly in the authentic researcher's place.

If the heuristic method is strictly applied, it disregards the teaching of experience and must inevitably slow up the pupil's progress. The conditions of school life do not permit of anything like the same expenditure of time on the discovery of a principle as was taken by the original discoverer. After observing the falling apple Newton is reputed to have taken nearly twenty years to formulate the law of gravity, and after the voyage of the *Beagle* it took Darwin a similar length of time to propound the theory of evolution. Even if these are extreme examples, original discoveries are made only after much trial and error, and not many children are likely to persevere in the face of repeated discouragement with all the time in the world at their disposal. Nearly 400 years ago Queen Elizabeth's tutor, Roger Ascham, observed that 'learning teacheth more in one year than experience in twenty', and that 'it is a marvellous pain to find out but a short way by long wandering'. In practice, no doubt, the heuristic teacher would intervene to head off the pupil from blind alleys and thus cause him to rehearse only the successful stages traversed by the discoverer in his quest for knowledge. But in that case it would be more accurate to regard heurism as a method of rediscovery than one of fresh discovery. To do so would not, of course, necessarily diminish its value for ordinary teaching purposes. The virtual impossibility of reconstructing the original situation is an even more serious difficulty in the thoroughgoing application of the heuristic method. In a world where the results of original discoveries are freely available, it assumes an artificial isolation which is quite unrealistic. In certain fields of abstract thought an occasional genius may genuinely achieve the kind of feat the advocates of heurism have in mind. We learn from the life of Blaise Pascal (1623–1662), by his elder sister, that at the age of twelve, without the help of any book, he independently worked out the early theorems of Euclid. Clearly, however, it would be absurd to credit the ordinary child with the requisite training and experience of the authentic discoverer. Even if he could discard at will his everyday experience, he could not be expected, like James Watt, to conceive the principle of the steam engine from simple observation of a boiling kettle.

Quite apart from these practical difficulties in fully implementing the heuristic method, there are a number of theoretical objections. The most cogent is doctrinaire insistence that the pupil must follow the precise order of the original discovery. This has the effect of introducing into a method primarily intended to be inductive a wholly unnecessary deductive element. In seeking to discover the working principles of a modern invention, a boy is more likely to find it natural to start from the present situation and reason back from effect to cause. In this respect, however, heurism adheres to the deductive procedure of reasoning from cause to effect, and its advocates would regard the 'how it works' method of teaching science as a grave deviation from orthodox principles. An objection of a less serious kind is that in genuine discovery proof is of the essence. It is said that a main reason why Darwin took so long to formulate his theory of evolution was the need for painstaking proof, once the fundamental idea had occurred to him. In the operation of the heuristic method, on the other hand, it is most unlikely that the child discoverer would ever be in a position to adduce the proof of any so-called discovery he might chance to make. It seems probable that even Armstrong realized that a thoroughgoing application of his method was impracticable. For, though he set his face against allowing overt knowledge to be given to pupils, he was prepared to concede that crystallized knowledge, in the shape of scientific instruments, might be made available to them.

To say this is not to deny the essential soundness of the heuristic principle or the beneficial effects of the heuristic movement. By giving greater scope for the exercise of individual initiative it allowed the teacher more freedom than traditional methods, and by recognizing the importance of pupil participation it afforded the learner something of the joy of discovery. Its most significant contribution was to bring home to pupil and teacher alike that for the full understanding of results, acquaintance with the process of acquiring knowledge is indispensable. In science teaching, in particular, this implied the substitution of practical and experimental instruction in place of the bookish and deductive teaching previously in vogue. The historical perspective implicit in the heuristic approach also encouraged specialists in other disciplines to take an interest in the history of their subjects. The value of this in preserving continuity between scientific theory and everyday practice is not always sufficiently appreciated. As James Ward points out:

Among the many qualifications of a first-rate teacher I should include this, a knowledge not only of his subject as it stands today but also of the steps by which it has been brought to that position. One of the reasons why the teaching even of science so often lacks the freshness and charm which men like Faraday and Hugh Miller could give it, is, I am inclined to think, that the teacher from the very first has known the science only in its latest phase (*Psychology Applied to Education*).

The heuristic method recognized the truth of this and endeavoured to supply the deficiency. It likewise brought an element of reality to the classroom which all too often was a completely novel experience.

Inductive methods presuppose a certain ingenuity of inference on the part of the learner and, therefore, underline the importance of conjecture in appropriate circumstances. Mere guesswork is often discouraged in the classroom, but it should be appreciated that guessing need not always be random or unintelligent. Indeed, the Gestalt psychologists have made it clear that much intelligent learning takes place by flashes of insight. Consequently, a lesson which leaves no room for guessing—or no unfilled gap for closure by the pupils—is hardly likely to give reasonable scope for enterprising thinking. If the pupils can answer every question with complete assurance, only two explanations are possible. Either the questions deal entirely with facts already known, in which case we have mere reproduction and not real thinking at all; or else they must be restricted to purely deductive subject-matter, in which case the thinking will be severely circumscribed. It will in fact be more or less limited to mathematical topics, for in no other subject can we expect to achieve the requisite precision from scanty data. On the other hand, when faced with analytical problems, pupils may often have no alternative but to rely on judicious guesswork to arrive at the desired solution. In this way much over-teaching is avoided, but at the same time the teacher must make it his business to ensure that the pupils are never discouraged by being presented with the kind of problem which may confront them with gaps that are beyond their capacity to close.

A variant of the heuristic principle is to be found in the problem or experimental method outlined by John Dewey in 1909 in a well-known work, *How We Think*. Though it seems unlikely that Armstrong's heurism exerted any immediate influence on Dewey's experimentalism, the problem method did in fact meet two of the shortcomings of the heuristic method. In it the problem is attacked directly instead of having to follow the order of discovery historically, and the testing of hypotheses is an important feature of the method. In his book Dewey is concerned with the implications of inductive reasoning for problem-solving, although he does not necessarily imply that no benefit is to be derived from studying how productive thinkers of the past proceeded in making their discoveries. As a basis for procedure in teaching, Dewey seeks to utilize an analysis of the thought process, and his main preoccupation is thus rather with *what* we do when engaged in thinking productively than with *how* productive thinking is actually carried on. In a sense the title of his book is somewhat misleading, for Dewey is not primarily concerned with giving a purely psychological account of the thought process. To illustrate his intention he cites in a chapter on the analysis of a complete act of thought three instances of extremely simple but genuine cases of reflective experience. They are taken from class papers written by his students, and in his view they provide appropriate material for analysing the thinking process into its constituent elements. In each case Dewey claims to discover five logically distinct steps. He rejects the traditional accounts of thinking as being abstract contemplation, or the direct result of sensation; for him it is the outcome of a challenge from the environment. Accordingly, the first step is what he calls a felt difficulty, or the consciousness of a problem. Secondly, we have the location and definition of the difficulty, or an analysis of the situation. Thirdly, we proceed to list suggestions for possible solutions of the problem. Fourthly, the implications of these various suggestions are developed by reasoning, with a view to selecting the most suitable. Finally, the proposed solution is tried out and either accepted or rejected in the light of further observation and experiment.

These five steps were discussed by Dewey in a more explicitly educational connection in *Democracy and Education* (1916). In his view the whole educative process centred in the provision of continuous activities in which the pupil is interested for their own sake. In the course of this activity a genuine problem must develop as a stimulus to thought. The pupil must then be put in possession of the requisite information and make the necessary observations for dealing with the problem. Next he has to assume responsibility for handling in an orderly fashion such solutions as may occur to him. Finally, to arrive at a valid judgment or conclusion, he requires sufficient opportunities for the experimental application and testing of his ideas. The essentially inductive character of Dewey's method is evident in the procedure from the statement of a problem, through the framing and testing of a hypothesis, to the elaboration of a principle or definition. Nevertheless, this has not prevented some people from making far-fetched comparisons with the Herbartian steps. We may perhaps concede a certain correspondence between the last two stages in the solution of a problem and the generalization and application steps in a Herbartian method unit. But there the resemblance ends, for the first two steps, and to a less extent the third, are quite dissimilar. In the case of the experimental method the pupil himself is expected to be aware of the problem, to discover independently those elements in his previous experience which will assist in dealing with it, and to think of appropriate solutions with very little help from the teacher. It was Dewey's belief that the method fostered in the pupil desirable personal traits which he designated directness, open-mindedness, single-mindedness and responsibility. Though he had in mind a strictly present reference rather than preparation for the future, Dewey held that the qualities developed by the successful application of his method had obvious relevance for adult life as well.

We may acknowledge the value of first-hand investigation and verification, and yet have reservations about the soundness of the experimental method as conceived by Dewey. As with the heuristic method, there is a strong possibility that a large number of wrong solutions will be tried out before the correct one is discovered. It may well be that faulty lines of action are not entirely fruitless, for clearly the experience so gained will be of some value in modifying the pupil's attitude on the next occasion. Indeed, for Dewey it was this very process of putting ideas to the test of experience that is truly educative, and he was at pains to require extensive opportunities for what he called purposive inquiry. Nevertheless, even he appreciated that mere repetitive activity could lose its purpose, and in such a case he was prepared to encourage teachers to show their pupils short cuts to the successful solution. The expedient he proposed was indirect control of the pupil through limitation of the environment. In effect this meant the fostering of internal control through participation in socialized activities, for Dewey was a firm believer in the value of these for producing identity of interest among pupils. He was convinced that suitable regulation of such activities by the teacher resulted in a greatly superior kind of direction to the physical compulsion of traditional methods. This aspect of his thinking was particularly stressed in the well-known Project Method, which was the logical outcome of Dewey's experimentalism.

We may perhaps also deplore Dewey's excessive emphasis on the vital importance of experimental activity in education. Without it there could be for him no 'real' knowledge whatever, with the result that purposive inquiry is permanently exalted at the expense of theoretical speculation. Dewey insisted that all productive thinking should satisfy two criteria: it must arise out of practical needs and it must issue in results that are tested by their consequences. Neither of these conditions is, however, essential in every case. Some problems arise out of pure intellectual curiosity while others may quite well be solved in imagination without any need for recourse to practical experiment. Oddly enough, Dewey himself is not consistent on this point. Of the three examples of reflective thinking which he instances only the first can be said to arise out of practical necessity and only the third involves an experimental solution. The remaining two arise out of curiosity or are solved by purely speculative activity. We must not, however, allow irrelevant considerations of this kind to influence our estimate of the value of Dewey's method for teaching purposes, nor indeed should it be inferred that practical necessity and experiment are in any sense out of place in the classroom. It may quite well be that the Project Method, which exploits so skilfully situations arising out of practical needs and necessitating the testing of results by practical application, owes its very success to Dewey's insistence that, for purposes of learning, productive thinking should involve both these features.

Suggestions for Further Reading:

Adams, Sir J., *Educational Movements and Methods*, Harrap, 1924.
Adamson, J. W., *English Education, 1789–1902*, C.U.P., 1930.
Armstrong, H. E., *The Teaching of Scientific Method*, Macmillan, 1903.
Curtis, S. J., *History of Education in Great Britain*, U.T.P., 1950.
Dewey, J., *Democracy and Education*, Macmillan, 1916.
Dewey, J., *How We Think*, Heath, 1910.
Rusk, R. R., *The Philosophical Bases of Education*, U.L.P., 1956.

THE PROJECT METHOD

No other specific teaching method has enjoyed so great a vogue as the Project Method. Though frequently attributed to Dewey himself, it is strictly speaking the creation of his colleague at Columbia University, W. H. Kilpatrick. Certainly the Project Method is a natural extension of Dewey's own teaching, and in *Democracy and Education* Dewey does once actually make incidental use of the term 'projects' in the chapter on play and work in the curriculum. It seems unlikely, however, that he intended it in quite the technical sense employed by Kilpatrick in his paper 'The Project Method: the Use of Purposeful Act in the Educative Process' which appeared in *Teachers College Bulletin* in October 1918. The element of novelty was that the new method proposed not merely the abstract solving of a problem but the whole sequence of activities involved in a complete undertaking. Thus, whereas Dewey had been chiefly concerned with applying inductive methods to the solution of an individual problem, e.g. the amount of wood required to construct a rabbit-hutch of a given size, this would now be regarded as part of an actual scheme for keeping livestock. The idea underlying the method was that children should develop their knowledge through trying out theories in the practical solution of problems, in the course of which they would come to appreciate the principles involved. The intention was also that fresh knowledge should be inculcated only as a result of the felt needs of the pupils. None of this was entirely new: project equivalents are advocated for the adolescent period by Rousseau in *Emile* (Bk. III); many of the activities prescribed by Froebel in *The Education of Man* for boyhood education are reminiscent of the project idea; and, as Sir Percy Nunn points out, the use of rural projects in the education of his own children is described by William Cobbett in his *Advice. to Young Men*.

Already in his problem method Dewey had derestricted heurism to the extent that the pupil was not necessarily bound to follow the method of the original discoverer. The Project Method seeks to go further in offering the pupil complete freedom of choice of problem to be solved, as well as of the means to be employed in solving it. The fundamental principle is the educative use of occupations that are suitably doctored to meet the requirements of the ordinary school. The result is that in place of externally imposed tasks of the traditional kind, the pupils' activities are centred round a number of spontaneous projects. As examples of straightforward projects might be mentioned the cultivation of land with the rotation of crops, the rearing of poultry with the necessary carpentry involved, or the production of a newspaper with the consequential technical skill in typesetting. Kilpatrick himself distinguished four main types of project designed to cover among them all aspects of ordinary school work, although obviously some overlap between one and another is inevitable. Thus he speaks of play projects where the dominant purpose is the acquirement of some item of knowledge or degree of skill, story projects in which the dominant purpose is to enjoy some aesthetic experience, excursion projects in which the dominant purpose is to solve some problem or to straighten out some difficulty, and hand projects where the dominant purpose is to embody some idea or plan in external form.

As envisaged by Kilpatrick, the scope of the Project was

intended to be extremely wide. In practice, however, in so far as his method was the outcome of Dewey's teaching, it tended to have particular reference to the kind of curriculum favoured by Dewey, which shows a bias towards the applied sciences and the industrial arts. Since teaching method must necessarily bear some relation to the content with which it deals, it follows that in the Project Method the procedure of the school is liable to be determined by the technique of the workshop. Again, as originally defined, a Project was a practical problem in its natural setting. But in fact the introduction of projects into schools may often necessitate abandonment of the natural setting. Consequently, so-called Projects are sometimes reduced to little more than practical problems, although Kilpatrick himself clearly regarded the treatment of theoretical questions, as well as appreciation of art and literature, as an essential function of the school. For him a Project may be said to represent a whole-hearted purposeful activity carried on in a social milieu, and he would be disposed to confine the term to this kind of activity, with due emphasis on its purpose. Kilpatrick's object, whether in carrying out a neighbourhood study or in scripting and staging a play or in building a boat, is always to bring the school, through the pupils' activities, into relation with life. It may well be that the informality of his approach affords the most satisfactory solution to this ticklish problem. Dewey, on the other hand, appears to favour a more realistic approximation: by attempting to equate a pupil's activity in a project with that of an apprentice learning his trade, he aims at an even closer relation to real life. Such thoroughgoing analogies are, however, not only unprofitable but, without fundamentally altering the character of a project, difficult to maintain. To be truly educative, a Project must afford genuinely spontaneous activity and at the same time generate corporate enthusiasm. In real life the apprentice all too often has restricted choice of employment and must work in an environment which does little to stimulate keenness to master the technique of his craft.

One of the earliest sustained trials of the Project Method was carried out in a rural school in Missouri, with two other rural schools serving as a control, by Kilpatrick's pupil, Ellsworth Collings. In 1923 Collings published an account of this in his work *An Experiment With a Project Curriculum*, and Kilpatrick availed himself of the opportunity to examine the underlying theory and to evaluate the results of his method in an introduction to the book. On the theoretical side he discerned four interrelated ideas which characterize the Project Method in operation. Firstly, Kilpatrick considered that if the school is to discharge its function properly, the pupils must purpose what they do. Secondly, he held that actual learning is never single—in the sense that it is always accompanied by what he called 'concomitant' learning of some kind, particularly in the building up of attitudes. Thirdly, he believed the right reason for encouraging learning by the pupils was that the instruction is currently required for the better execution of some enterprise already in hand. Fourthly, he regarded the curriculum as a series of guided exercises, related in such a way that what is learned in each of them is not isolated but serves to enrich the subsequent stream of experience. What is even more significant, however, is Kilpatrick's claim that these theoretical considerations were borne out in practice by four pragmatic results. The undoubted success of Collings's experiment amply demonstrated that a régime of child purposing was quite feasible. Increased enthusiasm, not only in school but at home, testified to the creation of new attitudes consistent with the theory. Even though much less attention was directed to results, testing of the gain in knowledge acquired proved the new procedure superior in inculcating conventional subject-matter. As the outcome of the experiment a new set of aims and new measures for estimating success were clearly indicated.

It must, of course, be plainly accepted that if education is to be carried on entirely by means of projects, certain consequences will flow. Not only will projects by their very nature cut across ordinary class-teaching and normal time-table arrangements, but they strike at the root of the conventional curriculum as well. A project takes a great deal of time and co-operative effort, and if it is to be restricted in the traditional fashion to so many isolated periods per week it must inevitably lack co-ordination. In the case of what Kilpatrick calls 'excursion' projects the usual time-table organization clearly goes by the board. Some of these administrative problems arise in connection with the use of films or wireless lessons or nature study walks in ordinary schools, but there are certain difficulties which are peculiar to the consistent application of the Project Method in practice. Two questions that obviously require consideration are whether the choice of project should be individual or co-operative in origin, and whether one and the same project can adequately cater for both individual and group needs. In practice there is a tendency for most projects to be teacher-dominated in origin, and for them to involve in execution the kind of activity that is group-motivated rather than that which arises out of the needs and values of individual pupils. The criticism here implied is that the Project Method may not make sufficient allowance for the growth of individuality in the child. One way of meeting this would be to leave to the pupils themselves complete freedom of choice in the activities to be undertaken.

If we do so, however, we run into further difficulties. Left entirely to their own devices, pupils will be deprived of the richer experience of adults; and this the monitorial system of the early nineteenth century plainly showed to be indispensable in children's education. Too much consideration for the individual may result in loss of the great social value to be derived from truly co-operative enterprises. More serious still is the risk of unco-ordinated activities, if the selection of the project is wholly at the discretion of the pupils. A choice made without any kind of central reference must obviously, more often than not, be largely an accidental one. It would, therefore, be quite unrealistic to depend upon chance whims and random happenings to provide a satisfactory scheme of education. Clearly, Kilpatrick himself was disposed to compromise on this issue. In the first instance he contemplated the collective choice of a project by the teacher and pupils jointly, but in the last resort the direction of this was to be vested solely in the teacher. It was envisaged that the teacher should have power either to sanction or to veto proposed lines of action and, indeed, the skilful use of suggestion on his part can go a long way towards obviating the disadvantages of decisions arbitrarily taken by children on their own. It was felt, too, that an experienced observer should have little difficulty in sensing intuitively the kind of stimulus for which the class as a whole feels a need. The most satisfying projects, nevertheless, are likely to arise out of common everyday experiences and inevitably these tend to cater for group activities rather than to gratify individual inclinations. Still, there must be something of value for every pupil in the co-operative work involved in conducting a regional survey in geography, in writing and producing a play in English, in cultivating a school garden in nature study, or even in planning a suitable colour scheme for decorating the school.

Another difficulty in the application of the Project Method is the possibility that the project selected may turn out to be too ambitious. That is to say, in practice it may well prove beyond the capacity of the pupils to bring to a successful conclusion. Should this happen, the outcome can only be discouragement and failure. Yet, if we may judge by pupils' efforts in the ordinary handwork lesson, they are quite often prone to overestimate their own executive capacity. In children there is a well-marked tendency to ignore Spencer's maxim about the need for working from the simple to the complex. On the other hand, if they are merely left to tackle a complex project which is clearly beyond their abilities, even though of their own choosing, they will in all likelihood very soon lose any interest in the particular activity. Admittedly, technical accuracy of finish is of less significance than encouragement of the creative impulse. For this reason it may sometimes be desirable to give the pupils their head, provided always that at the same time we do not allow them to be satisfied with inferior standards of work. In the last analysis, however, we must firmly lay the blame at the teacher's door if, by a process of trial and error, the pupils do not eventually learn to match their projects with their abilities and aptitudes. In this connection it is relevant to speculate to what extent, in the interests of free choice, the pupils should, like Rousseau's Emile, be required to devise their own apparatus. It may conceivably be argued that the use of instruments which are the products of the skill and experience of others, might have a limiting effect on individual freedom of action, although (as we have seen) not even Armstrong subscribed to this view. Nor do we find Dewey prepared to lend his support to this extreme requirement.

A problem of a rather different kind is the question of the pupil's age and stage of development. As children get older, their critical powers tend to outrun their executive skill, with the result that their own criticism of the products of their work may well inhibit them from undertaking fresh projects. This is essentially a problem of the adolescent period, but it suggests that the suitability of the Project approach may diminish after puberty. Younger children, on the other hand, though subject to discouragement, are not as a rule particularly critical of their creative efforts. In their case, even the intrinsic difficulty of the project selected may well have a less disheartening effect than the sheer length of time required to complete it. The fact is that young children, although often capable of sustained effort while engaged on constructive work, generally also have a relatively short interest span. What they look for is a quick return for effort expended, and so they are usually quite satisfied with relatively crude results. The moral here is that for these younger children a project that is long-drawn-out, even though initially interesting and well within their capacity, may easily begin to lose its appeal after two or three weeks. The converse, of course, also holds good, namely that some projects, by reason of their restricted time span, are necessarily too superficial to be educative in any real sense.

In the hands of the undiscerning teacher the Project Method is, accordingly, open to a number of abuses. Projects may, for instance, be adopted or abandoned with too easy complacency. They may be allowed to serve as little more than a pleasurable means of filling in time, rather as crossword puzzles too often engross the attention of adults whose energies might more profitably be engaged on truly productive tasks. On occasion they may even act as a kind of defence mechanism against having to face up to the challenge of real situations. Clearly, therefore, if projects have nothing more to offer than surrogate activities, there can be no question of looking on them, as Dewey would have us do, as the school counterparts of industrial life. Indeed, it is fair to say that one of the more obvious shortcomings in the case of the Project Method is its very need to absorb some of the discipline implicit in the social and economic constraints that are characteristic of jobs in industry. The most serious difficulty in the successful application of the Project Method is, however, the problem of ensuring any kind of systematic progress. It is not only that the choice of the subject-matter itself is liable to be accidental; the actual learning of the selected material is also likely to be incidental. When properly motivated, incidental learning has its due place in the process of education, but intentional learning is in general far more efficient. With incidental learning a great deal of value is apt to be overlooked in any branch of study. Moreover, some highly systematic subjects, such as mathematics, simply do not respond at all to incidental treatment. In a case of this kind it is surely more realistic for the teacher to recognize quite frankly that he has little option but to follow the order indicated by the development of the subject-matter, rather than that suggested by the whim of his pupils.

One of Dewey's main objections to the traditional treatment of school subjects was over-emphasis on drill, or (as he put it) getting a tool for subsequent use. To some extent the Project Method has followed him in this matter. Knowledge is not to be stored for future requirements but is sought merely to deal with a current emergency. This is all very well, but in practice it is difficult to see how a certain amount of 'over-learning' in the tool subjects of the curriculum can in fact really be avoided. If the pupil's mind is to be freed to deal later with the complexities of language, mathematics and science, he will obviously require a greater facility in the basic processes than he is likely to achieve merely by looking things up incidentally for reference. We may conclude, then, that the Project Method in no sense absolves the teacher from the need for acquainting himself with the techniques of the basic school subjects. Indeed, it is very far from being a lazy man's method. Kilpatrick freely admitted that at an early stage in his experiment Collings found the reverse to be true. For success in schools run on this basis the requisite conditions demanded more in the way of buildings and equipment, more ability, zeal and preparation on the part of teachers, more science and a higher art in the work itself than was needed in other schools. Deceptively easy though the Project Method may superficially appear, it can be fittingly described in the well-known words of John Milton: 'This is not a bow for every man to shoot in that counts himself a teacher' (*Tractate of Education*). On the contrary, we must expect that the consistent employment of such methods will call for more highly qualified teachers and a more generous staffing ratio than traditional programmes of teaching. On the whole, experience appears to indicate the greater suitability of the Project approach at the primary stage, but it would be a mistake to allow this finding to blind us to its possibilities later on. There seems little doubt that the impetus gained from success in earlier projects can be put to good use by a skilful teacher in tackling the specialist subjects of the secondary school.

So far we have been mainly concerned with some of the difficulties and limitations of the Project Method as a medium of teaching; these should not be permitted to obscure its advantages. If there is any substance in Dewey's analogy between the pupil and a craftsman, it stands to reason that a project will enable the former to survey his problem realistically as a whole. The very possibility of this invests it for him with a significance which is so often lacking in ordinary school work. It is true, certainly, that such wholes are sometimes rather fortuitous or arbitrary, and that a conspectus of them may not therefore always be pure gain. Nevertheless, projects as such are seldom arbitrary to the same degree as the topics treated in the traditional school. Against this it may be argued that conventional school subjects, if properly taught, can also be seen as wholes, and even that they have an added advantage of system and permanence that is lacking in a project. The difficulty here, however, is to get pupils to see them in this light by the use of traditional methods. Still, it has to be admitted that the education given by projects is likely to emphasize relationships in breadth rather than in depth. By this is meant that while the educative effects will tend to be integration of the various elements of the pupil's experience into a well-knit whole, it is only at the expense of some loss of consolidation within each individual element. Another argument in favour of the Project Method is that it encourages pupil participation in planning the work from beginning to end. Traditional methods, on the other hand, as a rule leave merely the routine or mechanical aspects to be dealt with by the pupil. Yet it should be frankly recognized that only if the pupil himself is allowed to propose the design of an experiment, is he likely to have sufficient opportunity to develop the initiative and self-criticism on which all progress depends.

As a consequence of its practical and social implications the Project Method has the advantage of conferring on school work a much-needed sense of reality. To a considerable extent it does in fact seem to succeed in relating what goes on in school to the actualities of life. In the modern world, with a progressive increase in the length of school life, this is an important consideration. Pedagogically, the Project Method appears to accord well with the psychological concept of maturation. That is to say, it provides the pupil with the sort of learning material that suits his particular stage of mental development. The more mature pupils are likely to go for the abstract and difficult features of the task in hand and leave the simple elements to the others. Without holding up learning altogether this does permit postponement of the teaching of formal subjects until the emergence of felt needs. Finally, the wholesome moral effects of the successful operation of the Project Method must be mentioned. There can be no doubt that participation in a co-operative enterprise develops an enhanced sense of responsibility in children. Whole-hearted devotion to the project of the moment cumulatively supplies a valuable moral training that the formalized atmosphere of the ordinary classroom makes much more difficult to foster.

The theoretical basis on which the Project Method is built up differs little from that originally formulated for experimentalism. Like Dewey, Kilpatrick recognizes five stages in the development of what he considers a genuine project. These are regarded, however, less as 'steps' in the

ически chronological sense than as 'logical phases' in dealing with an actual situation. First, then, an actual situation
is to be devised. This must at once have inner meaning
for the pupil and provide him with external motivation to
action. Generally it will require to be very largely impro-
vised by the teacher personally. Next, it is the pupil's
business to analyse the situation, with a view both to determining ends and deciding on means for dealing with it.
Then comes the planning stage, which at this juncture can
be only tentative and flexible if the situation is to be allowed
to develop satisfactorily. Here imaginative treatment is
called for, although at the same time imagination must have
regard to hard facts. The next stage involves putting the
plan into operation. The important point here is to maintain
constant vigilance to ensure that it is going to work, or to
make any necessary readjustment as the need arises. All that
now remains is for the learner, on successful completion of
the project, to evaluate what has been accomplished and,
in particular, to assess in what way this might be improved
on a future occasion.

The carrying through of a project, if we may omit the
first stage as mainly the teacher's contribution, thus implies
on the pupil's part a fourfold act of purposing, planning,
executing and judging. Even so, on more than one occasion
we find Dewey expressing distinct misgivings as to the
adequacy of projects from the strictly educational point of
view. For a project to be considered educationally valuable
he lays down certain definite requirements which it must
fulfil. It must, for instance, clearly engage the learner's
interest. Otherwise, even if externally he may appear to be
persevering with his task, his mind will revolt from it. Then
again it must involve intrinsically worthwhile activity, even
though from an adult point of view the final outcome need
not necessarily be useful. In the course of its development
it must also present problems that awaken new curiosity in
the pupil and create a demand for fresh information on his

part. Finally, if it is to avoid a mere succession of unrelated activities and ensure proper continuity, it must cover a sufficient time-span. Unless a project meets all these conditions Dewey would pronounce it valueless. We may, however, concede that the training in the way of organizing knowledge that is furnished by the mere process of assembling individual contributions to almost any completed project, is likely to be more immediately valuable than a great deal of formal knowledge simply gained at second hand.

Whatever may be the spirit underlying the work, it is not strictly accurate to classify the Project Method as one of the so-called 'play-way' methods of teaching. This description, originally applied by Caldwell Cook to dramatic methods of teaching English, has gradually come to designate any method that employs the play activities of children to further their own education. It would be a mistake to regard such activities as frivolous, or to deny the possibility of securing serious work by a proper direction of play. Nevertheless, the orthodox adherents of the Project Method incline, at least in the case of older children, to view a project as a replica in the school of the serious business of life. While, therefore, we may regard the Project Method as a worthy expression of the practical genius of the American people, we must attribute to it something of the 'life is real, life is earnest' philosophy of their best-known poet. In the field of infant education, it is true, some modification of the full significance of a project is considered permissible. Here, indeed, a project is looked on quite frankly as pure play activity. The reason for this differentiation is, no doubt, that the spontaneous activities of the kindergarten involve both work and play, and any attempt to distinguish sharply between them would be futile. Nevertheless, even at the infant stage, it is customary to credit the use of the Project Method with at least two of the more serious virtues claimed for it in the case of older children.

Like the gifts and occupations of Froebel or the didactic apparatus of Montessori, it affords an acceptable means of postponing the provision of formal instruction until such time as the pupils are ready for it. Secondly, it presents young children entering school, who for the most part tend to be sturdy little individualists, with unrivalled opportunities for acquiring social training.

Certainly the pragmatic approach to knowledge offered by the Project Method is well suited to the young child's stage of mental development. Other inductive methods are apt to stop short at merely appreciating the way in which new principles are discovered. The Project Method, however, encourages pupils to achieve a deeper insight into such principles through actually seeing them in operation. The chief limitation to which it is subject, in this respect, is the particular area of the school curriculum in which the development of projects can be regarded as really natural. In formal subjects like mathematics, science and languages it is difficult to devise projects that are not forced. In social studies, dramatic work and art, on the other hand, they are likely to seem much less artificial.

Suggestions for Further Reading:

Adams, Sir J., *Modern Developments in Educational Practice*, U.L.P., 1928.

Boyd, W., *The History of Western Education*, Black, 1921.

Collings, E., *An Experiment with a Project Curriculum*, Macmillan, 1923.

Kilpatrick, W. H., *Foundations of Method*, Macmillan, 1925.

Nunn, Sir T. P., *Education: Its Data and First Principles*, Arnold, 1945.

Thomson, G. H., *A Modern Philosophy of Education*, Allen & Unwin, 1929.

CHAPTER V

THE ROLE OF INTEREST IN LEARNING

WHILE it may be true that the Project Method does not directly seek to utilize the play energies of children, it certainly depends for its success on engaging their interest. What the precise nature of interest in this sense may be, is not always easy to determine. All we can say with confidence is that in practice it involves securing the co-operation of the pupils in a worthwhile task. It may not, indeed, be essential or even possible to enlist the highest motives, and we can be reasonably satisfied in many cases if we see our efforts result in vigorous activity on their part. In the sphere of interest Sir Percy Nunn suggests a dual purpose for the teacher: to enable the child to face the world with increasing independence and richer relationship, and, more important, to enable him to express himself in activities of increasing value. This implies that the teacher's task involves not only the use in the actual business of teaching of whatever interests his pupils may have, but the cultivation of others that are likely to be of value to him in his development towards maturity. Whether we employ deductive or inductive methods, interest must be regarded as an essential constituent of all successful teaching. Since, however, the project in particular is so dependent on this factor for the initiation of activity on the part of the learners, it may be well now to consider what its advocates have to say about what they call the doctrine of interest. More than a century ago Herbart strove to base instruction upon interest, and his views were popularized in this country by Sir John Adams in *The Herbartian Psychology Applied to Education* (1897). Even Dewey in his early days wrote a pamphlet for the American Herbartian Society, called *Interest as Related to Will* (1896), which was republished as *Interest and Effort in Education* in 1913. Kilpatrick drew extensively on this for his three chapters on interest in *Foundations of Method*; in this work he discusses the three components which go to make up 'what we may call the doctrine of interest'. He defines them as a gripping interest, a challenge from the situation for the best effort that in us lies, and eventual success.

The main problem is, of course, how to arouse this gripping interest in the first instance. This is no new problem and educators throughout the centuries have noted the importance of interest for stimulating the activity of learning. Plato, for instance, in discussing the studies preliminary to dialectic in *The Republic*, suggests that they should be set before the prospective rulers, as boys, in such a fashion as not to make them seem compulsory. Study forced on the mind will not abide there, he says, and children are better trained by games than by compulsion. Even the Puritan educators of the seventeenth century stress the need for non-coercive methods of teaching. John Dury, in *The Reformed School* (1650), urged teachers to make nothing tedious and grievous to children but so to prepare everything for their benefit that the work should be to them 'as a delightful recreation by the variety and easiness thereof'. The proper attitude to be inculcated in the pupils he rather quaintly described as being 'to make them affectionate towards the task which is to be offered unto them, that is, attentive and greedy to receive it'. This may, perhaps, be too much to hope for, but there can be no doubt that such an outlook is greatly preferable to the punishment avoidance that often characterizes classroom activity. The latter,

though not necessarily ineffective, cannot but leave unpleasant associations in the pupil's mind. While application
may not always be lacking, it is unlikely that the results of
learning under conditions of this kind will be so permanent
as in the case of pupils who have a positive interest in the
task. Moreover, the negative effect of the use of penalties is
bound to colour a pupil's whole attitude to the subject of
study, to the teacher himself and even to school work in
general.

On the other hand, the stimulating influence of utilizing
the interest of the moment is cogently expressed in the well-
known words of Rousseau: 'Present interest, that is the
motive power, the only motive power which takes us far and
safely' (*Emile*, Bk. II). Pestalozzi, also, equated want of
application in children with lack of interest, the blame for
which he was inclined to attribute as often as not to the
teacher himself. For Herbart, interest was much more
closely linked with instruction, and in his view the sole
means of evoking it consisted in selecting the right subject-
matter, and adopting the right method of presenting this.
In other words, if interest is to be aroused, not only must
the teacher in the presentation of his material follow the
Herbartian steps but the mind of the pupil must act 'apper-
ceptively' in response to his instruction. Dewey describes
interest as 'the absence of a gulf' between the material of
study and the mind of the pupil. Presumably he means by
this that if interest is present, the pupil's mental powers
should automatically find themselves at home with the particular subject-matter. Put the other way round, the feeling
of alienation often experienced when the attention is forcibly
directed to subject-matter that is foreign to one's personal
experience, is the converse of interest in Dewey's sense of
the word.

It is questionable, however, whether the observations of
these writers greatly clarify the true nature of interest in
its educational reference for us today. At one time 'soft

pedagogy' was a favourite reproach of those who decried appeal to interest in any form in the teaching of the young. Nowadays we are generally enlightened enough to concede that interest of some kind is an essential concomitant of learning. What we have still to decide is whether this interest is to be derived from extrinsic or intrinsic considerations. A good deal of reliance has traditionally been placed on extrinsic factors, such as marks and prizes, but modern activity methods have done much to show that intrinsic concern for the work itself may in the long run be a superior dynamic. It might be supposed that in such a matter the reactions of pupils would be as fully considered as the opinions of educationists. Until relatively recently, however, surprisingly little information was available on this point. A report of the National Foundation for Educational Research, published in 1952 with the title *A Survey of Rewards and Punishments in Schools*, is probably the most exhaustive investigation of the field. With its findings on the negative question of penalties we are not concerned, but on the positive side it does serve to throw fresh light on the problem of interest as a motive force in the classroom. As a result of extensive inquiries into existing practice the two investigators, Miriam Highfield and A. Pinsent, contrived to draw up a list of twelve potential incentives. They then endeavoured to obtain opinions as to the relative effectiveness of these from a representative sample both of secondary teachers and of senior pupils taught by them.

To this end they circularized 94 secondary schools (grammar, technical and modern) in both urban and rural areas. Replies were received from 959 teachers (including men and women heads and assistants) and from 7309 pupils between 11 and 15 years of age (both boys and girls). In addition to the conventional award of prizes, the kind of incentives included by the investigators in their questionnaire embraced the following: class outings, favourable reports for home, good marks for written work, doing well in a test, temporary leadership in games or class, public praise, quiet appreciation by the teacher, credit gained for team or house in class work or sports, election by fellow-pupils or appointment by the teacher as prefect. The teachers were asked to rank these various incentives in order of importance for preserving what they considered good morale, and the pupils to rank them in the order in which the different incentives appealed most to them. Answers to an inquiry of this kind must necessarily be subjective in nature, and so the results obtained can in no sense be regarded as experimentally established. Nevertheless, rankings among teachers (whether heads or assistants) on the one hand, and among pupils (whether boys or girls) on the other, did show a remarkable agreement. At the same time there was a significant disparity of opinion between the two groups.

The teachers considered quiet appreciation, appointment to a position of authority, and election to leadership by fellow-pupils to be the most powerful incentives, and, oddly enough, they tended to rate tangible rewards, like prizes and class outings, at the bottom of the scale. The pupils, on the other hand, seemed to value most a favourable report for home, doing well in a test, and credit gained for team or house in sports and class work. They appreciated least positions of leadership (whether appointed by the teachers or elected by their fellow-pupils) and public praise. The clear inference to be drawn from these findings is that the teachers appeared to be thinking in terms of adult approval whereas the pupils had in mind, rather, successful personal achievement. Since opportunities for appointment to leadership are inevitably restricted, the latter would appear to be the more realistic viewpoint. Furthermore, if due allowance is made for individual differences in capacity, there seems to be no reason why satisfactory progress should not lie within the reach of all. We cannot, of course, be sure that what pupils profess to prefer will necessarily get the best out of them, but clearly teachers must take into account any incentive that plainly appeals to children. Their chief concern as pupils appears to be success in their work in relation to their own particular ability. If, then, a more serious attempt were made to match with greater accuracy the task set with the capacity of the individual, we might reasonably expect the natural interest in successful achievement to prompt every pupil to furnish his best effort. What does seem certain is that a purely extrinsic system of marks is most unlikely either to stimulate the right kind of effort or to correct the common failings of laziness, carelessness and inattention.

If the essential nature of interest remains elusive, we can at least clear up some misconceptions, such as the tendency to identify the interesting with what is easy, pleasurable, or amusing. This confusion is a grave, if common, mistake. It is a matter of everyday observation, for instance, that children show a preference for activities that demand some exertion. The Outward Bound movement is designed to cater for the spirit of adventure in adolescents by presenting them with challenging situations, and even in the recreational activities of adults artificial hazards are sometimes introduced as a means of enhancing interest in the game or sport. For most children school work is inherently difficult enough, but delinquency arising out of boredom is by no means unknown among abler pupils. Even Herbart shrewdly recognized that too easy instruction merely causes ennui, and in practice it will generally be found that interest intensifies, rather than eliminates, effort. Somewhat similar considerations apply to confusing the interesting with the pleasurable. Genuine satisfaction, rather than mere pleasure, should be our aim. It is not the object of the play way, for example, to reduce all school work to play, nor does the doctrine of interest seek to eliminate all drudgery from education. What it does set out to do, wherever possible, is to invest such drudgery with meaning. In the past the moral value of mere hard grind has undoubtedly been exaggerated by educational writers; even so stern a moralist as Kant, while distrustful of pleasure, was prepared to concede that, in addition to pure virtue, an element of happiness enters into the complete moral good.

No doubt the ideal to be aimed at in the matter of interest is the wholehearted devotion to a set task that characterizes the Project Method at its best. Any interest aroused must, however, always be sincere, for simulated interest in an inherently uncongenial task generates nothing but hypocrisy. Further evidence of the fallacy of identifying the interesting with the pleasurable is to be found in the spontaneous interest evoked by painful or unpleasurable experiences, such as tragedy. Still less justification exists for confusing interest with amusement. The value of an occasional flash of humour for leavening an otherwise dull topic will be readily admitted, but interest in the true sense cannot be secured by the purely adventitious means dear to the comedian. There is a suggestion of idle diversion in the idea of amusement, which must surely reduce the school to a kind of circus and put the teacher rather on the level of a clown. It is not even adequate to look on interest as just the harmless sugar coating that gilds the educational pill. We must have a much more positive conception of its role in learning. Properly regarded, it is an effect rather than a cause; it is the outcome, far more than the agent, of good teaching. At the same time, the teacher would clearly not be justified in employing the means at his disposal to create a purely volatile interest in what may turn out to be merely a passing phase. In this respect he must be careful to sift the wheat from the chaff.

Some of these misconceptions are in a large measure due to the failure to differentiate between two quite distinct types of interest. On the one hand we have the fleeting primitive interests directly based on innate tendencies, on the other the more stable acquired interests that imply a social reference. Plainly the teacher's function must not be limited to the mere gratification of the pupil's innate tendencies; it should seek by a process of 'sublimation' to transform these into activities of social value. In practice, this means that, instead of being afforded crude expression in the form of primitive interests, the impulses which derive from these innate tendencies must often be redirected into socially valuable channels, from which they will emerge in a more refined form as acquired interests. Accordingly, although the teacher is constantly urged to stimulate the child's native curiosity, his aim is not simply to satisfy idle inquisitiveness. Rather, his object will be to encourage the development of long-term interests in various aspects of knowledge. If the pupil's simple questions about 'what God is like', or 'what the world is made of', are sympathetically handled, we may reasonably hope that a stable interest in theology or physics will, in some cases at least, eventually develop. Such cases are no doubt exceptional, but the fact remains that one of the most important objects of schooling must always be the cultivation of interests that will continue to develop once school-days are over. Those who deprecate the use of interest in teaching are, accordingly, generally thinking in terms of the primitive type of interest, which at best can afford only temporary satisfaction. The advocates of the doctrine of interest, on the other hand, have in view the acquired type of interest. For them the success of instruction is to be measured less by the quantity of knowledge imparted than by the strength of the interest created in the pupil. The essential difference between one type and the other is that an acquired interest, once initiated, is self-sustaining, whereas primitive interests soon flag. They require to be constantly reinforced by appeals to duty, promises of reward, or threats of punishment.

One of the empirical laws of teaching is: arouse interest and you will secure attention. Here it is clearly primitive interest that is, in the first instance at least, mainly referred to, although merely to get hold of the pupils' attention at the beginning of the lesson is not in itself the whole story. On the other hand, there is no doubt that the use of material primarily appealing to innate tendencies does effectively stimulate the will to learn in the young. We are well on the way to eventual success if, at a given moment, we can only get the learner to identify what is presented with the current tendencies at work in his own mind. Just how this identification is to be brought about is the core of the problem. The Herbartian educators, as we have seen, made great play with the need for raising at the psychological moment appropriate ideas to consciousness. For this they relied on the principle of 'apperception', which was for them perception of a special kind at a higher level of mental activity. Ordinary sensory perception depends not only on the immediate sense data that are present, but on the partial reinstatement of previous sensory experience of a relevant kind. Thus, the artist will 'see' more in a landscape, or the musician will 'hear' more in a melody, than the man in the street, because each will tend to add to the basic data an interpretative element from his previous visual or auditory experience. In much the same way apperception, at the ideational level, depends, it is claimed, on an appropriate background of mental experience to facilitate the reception of new material into the mind. This frame of reference Herbart called an 'apperception mass' and upon its presence at the requisite time hinged the whole effectiveness of any piece of instruction. In the absence of such a background a new idea may conceivably be apprehended in rote fashion but it will not be comprehended in any real sense.

A certain amount of basic instruction, it is true, may have to be imparted in this way from sheer necessity, but if great care is not afterwards taken to relate it to the existing content of the growing mind it cannot be expected to have any permanence. Moreover, it is not unlikely that unrelated instruction of this kind may be misinterpreted in the light of such limited, though irrelevant, experience as the pupil may already have at his disposal. Thus, the pupil who defines the equator as 'a menagerie lion' running round the earth, or the boy who murmurs 'Harold be Thy name' when repeating the Lord's Prayer, is merely doing his best to interpret unfamiliar ideas in terms of his own experience. It might not be so bad if the teacher merely had a complete void to contend with. So often, however, a more or less incongruous frame of reference already exists in the pupils' minds, against which he must try to project his ideas. To the art master 'a good picture' may mean a painting of merit, whereas to the majority of his pupils it is more likely to suggest an exciting film. Sometimes this may result in an unintentionally humorous situation, where out-of-school experiences accidentally impinge on the work of the class-room. If the geography teacher asks where Burnley is, for instance, he may receive the reply 'at the top of the league'. Clearly a frame of reference exists, but for his purposes it is an irrelevant one associated with sport instead of the cotton industry. A resourceful teacher would, no doubt, turn an unexpected situation of this kind to advantage by utilizing the pupils' interest in the football team as a focus on which to direct attention to the town whose name it bears.

The reverse process of deliberately projecting ideas against an incongruous background is the basis of intentionally humorous situations as seen in many jokes. A canny Aberdonian, approached by a tramp for 'sixpence for a bed', asks to see the bed. The whole point here depends upon projection of business acumen against the improbable background of impecuniousness. There is nothing startlingly novel in the principle of apperception, for recognition of the need for preparing an appropriate background for the reception of fresh ideas dates back to the time of Socrates. The significance of Herbart's so-called 'discovery' of the apperception mass for educational advance has, accordingly, been variously estimated. Some profess to see in it a major contribution to educational psychology, others regard it as merely a straightforward account of what takes place when anything new enters the mind without really enlightening us as to how this happens. Herbart can probably claim some credit for the clarity with which he perceived that fresh facts can be interpreted only in the light of a given individual's existing mental content. Thus the mere presentation of an object or an idea to a class of pupils is no guarantee, as is so often assumed, that it will automatically become an organized part of their knowledge. E. A. Peel, writing on learning as insight, elucidates as follows:

Also aiding clarity of form is the experience of the observer. He tends to give meaning to configurations set before him in terms of what he has learned and is interested in. This condition seems to be very close to what Herbart called apperception. The experience was called the 'apperception mass'. Our present perceptions are governed to some extent by our knowledge and attitudes (*The Psychological Basis of Education*).

It should, of course, be recognized that it is possible to place excessive reliance on the old as a means of interpreting the new. Familiarity proverbially breeds contempt, and excessive adherence to the teaching maxim of always proceeding from the known to the unknown may well result in superficiality of knowledge. The most likely occasion for such an occurrence is the ingestion of fresh material which is insufficiently analysed because of close analogy with material that is already there. In any branch of study where technical terms are already known to the pupils in a very general sense, the introduction of specialized terminology is a case in point. In physics, for instance, many of the terms are also found in everyday use, e.g. force. Unless some care is taken, when they first occur in the new context, to present them in an appropriate frame of reference, their special significance may well escape the learners. On the other hand, it may be conceded that the apparent absence of the requisite apperception mass can sometimes have its uses. A uniform blank in the minds of his pupils should serve as a warning to the perceptive teacher that presentation of the idea he is expounding is either premature or inopportune. Pestalozzi had endeavoured to explain the transformation of clear images, gained by the child from immediate experience of objects and situations, into definite ideas by the complex process which he called 'Anschauung'. Herbart sought to complete this account of mental growth by adding an essential interpretative element derived from former experiences.

The educational implications of such experiences are extremely important. The apperception masses to which they give rise have a relational bearing on the pupil's mental range as well as affecting the mind's content at any given stage. Not only do they determine what is actually present. They may also determine the degree of complexity with which he will ultimately be able to deal with new ideas in related fields of knowledge. For example, whatever a child's native ability and however efficient his subsequent instruction in mathematics may be, undue restriction of his early experience of number may permanently impair the effectiveness of his grasp of scientific concepts. Apperception for Herbart was essentially cognitive in character, whereas interest in the modern sense has come to be regarded as more closely bound up with the emotional side of mental life. H. A. Murray's *Thematic Apperception Test*, a projective test for the assessment of personality, retains Herbart's term in its title, and the technique of free association used in psycho-analysis is in a sense an application of the apperception mass to therapeutic purposes. Attempts have even been made to construct vocabulary tests involving association as a means of determining children's scholastic interests. They take the form of word-lists of homonyms, suitable for administering to pupils in the 10 to 11 year old range, having both theoretical and practical associations. By the meanings which pupils attach to the words in such vocabulary tests, they often reveal their interests in either academic or technical matters. In conjunction with other data, this information can be of some value in allocating those concerned to the most suitable type of secondary education. Nevertheless, the development of an enduring interest is likely to depend as much on knowledge as on emotional disposition.

Suggestions for Further Reading:

Adams, Sir J., *The Herbartian Psychology Applied to Education*, Heath, 1897.
Caldwell Cook, H., *The Play Way*, Heinemann, 1917.
Kilpatrick, W. H., *Foundations of Method*, Macmillan, 1925.
Kilpatrick, W. H., *Philosophy of Education*, Macmillan, 1951.
McFarland, H. S. N., *Psychology and Teaching*, Harrap, 1958.
National Foundation for Educational Research, *Survey of Rewards and Punishments in Schools*, Newnes, 1952.
Peel, E. A., *The Psychological Basis of Education*, Oliver & Boyd, 1956.
Rusk, R. R., *The Doctrines of the Great Educators*, Macmillan, 1954.

CHAPTER VI

THE PLACE OF SUGGESTION
IN TEACHING

BOTH deductive and inductive methods tend to presuppose that what is to be taught can be communicated more or less directly to the pupils. So long as we are dealing with straightforward school subjects, such as mathematics, science, or geography, this is no doubt the case, but we must not overlook those aspects of the curriculum which are popularly said to be 'caught' rather than taught. Of particular importance in this respect is the moral and religious side of education, which obviously cannot be treated in the same way as purely factual knowledge. It was Keatinge's contention that in all effective teaching an element of each of his 'triad of essential methods' is present, although the proportions may vary from one branch of knowledge to another. The whole art of the teacher, he believed, lay in finding the exact blend of the three ingredients that best suited his subject, his pupils and himself. In the subjects of the curriculum that are predominantly ethical he saw the greatest scope for the use of suggestion. This was hardly a new pedagogical discovery, for the poet Alexander Pope was well aware that 'men must be taught as if you taught them not'. The point Keatinge is at pains to make, however, is that the apperceptive process which we have just discussed can be initiated in the pupil's mind by indirect, as well as direct, methods of presentation. This indirect method is through the use of suggestion, which contrives to mediate between the directly imposed authority of demonstration and the largely uncontrolled activity of heurism. Control which can be exercised without the pupil's consciousness of it is a valuable medium in the hands of the teacher.

Nevertheless, there has always been some hesitation in advocating unreservedly the use of suggestion in teaching. There are probably two main reasons for this cautious point of view. In the first place, the imitation which is induced by suggestion was long regarded as characteristic of the childish and immature mind. Now, although it is more readily acknowledged that we are all to some extent imitators, there is still a tendency in orthodox circles to deprecate 'suggestive' methods. A more powerful reason, however, is the fear of indoctrination. The long-standing association of suggestion with hypnotic phenomena has undoubtedly rendered it suspect in the public mind. In an extreme form suggestion may sometimes be the instrument for communicating to other people beliefs and attitudes without trying to convince them of any logical grounds for their acceptance. We have all heard of subliminal advertising, and totalitarian régimes do not scruple to utilize mass media for deliberately indoctrinating youth in this way. But the modified use of suggestion approved by the genuine educator is a very different matter. It is in fact nothing more than the exercise of a mild external suasion to bring into action, and to influence in a desired direction, ideational systems that are already latent in the pupil's mind.

In the psychological process known as social induction, suggestion is now recognized as a perfectly respectable component, and in this sense it is generally regarded as a quite legitimate channel for exerting personal influence in teaching. Indeed it often has a positive advantage over direct communication, if only because apperceptive systems once set in motion by means of it have a tendency to go on automatically. An idea implanted in a pupil's mind by suggestion appears to him as his own and for that reason acquires greater power and significance. We may admit that to some extent inductive teaching, by enlisting the pupil's active co-operation, already recognizes this principle. Armstrong's heurism and Kilpatrick's project no doubt incorporate a covert suggestive influence that makes its appeal. When we are concerned with a more overt use of suggestion in teaching, we must, however, be careful to observe a certain subtlety of technique. If we fail to do so, the suggested idea is liable to miscarry and so to lose its effect on the pupil. In this connection two precautions seem particularly desirable. The further back the external impulse can be thrown, the more likely the pupil will be to believe that he is acting on his own initiative. In other words, it is rarely sufficient to try to superimpose a new ethical idea on the child's immediate experience. What the skilful teacher has to do is to probe into the pupils' past experience and attempt to associate it with the incidents of early childhood. Secondly, the more obliquely the suggestion can be presented, the greater will be its chances of successful assimilation in the pupil's mind. If, for example, we wish to convey the idea that stealing is anti-social, a concrete instance that 'crime doesn't pay' will probably be more effective than a direct appeal to right or wrong.

It is only by astute prior questioning on the moral bearing of such concrete situations that the teacher can prepare the ground for acceptance of the idea itself. Once this has been implanted in the pupil's mind, however, the answers to subsequent questions, being his own, help to carry greater conviction of its force. Thus it is in the sphere of suggestion that the so-called 'teaching' question is of greatest importance. The distinction between a question of this kind and one of the examining type is that its function is rather to implant ideas than to test knowledge. For this reason it need not always conform to the more rigid conventions governing ordinary classroom questioning. Even rhetorical questions may be justified for such a purpose, nor is there in the case of 'teaching' questions the same objection to accepting answers in plain yes or no form, e.g. do you think capital punishment is compatible with the sixth commandment? This does not imply that great care should not be exercised in framing the actual questions put, for even a slight variation in the form of a question may enormously enhance its suggestive power. In this connection it is perhaps not without significance that the recorded discourse of two great moral teachers of antiquity, namely Socrates and Christ himself, reveals great skill in the delicate art of using questions as a means of making others clarify their own hazy ideas.

Suggestion is usually an influence which emanates from some external source, such as the teacher, and this kind is designated hetero-suggestion. Suggestion may, however, originate from within the individual himself and it is then known as auto-suggestion. In that case, whether the idea be spontaneous or deliberate in nature, the pupil's response must inevitably be a positive one. The same cannot, unfortunately, be said of his reaction to hetero-suggestion, which is often just as likely to be negative. There are, nevertheless, certain fairly well defined conditions in which response to hetero-suggestion is best calculated to be positive, although these are not always relevant to the classroom. The relative dissociation characteristic of fatigue or certain abnormal mental states offers the hypnotist or propagandist a particularly favourable opportunity for exploiting the individual for his own ends. Nazi youth rallies, it is said, were deliberately held in the late evening in order to maximize the dissociative effects of fatigue as a means of enhancing adolescent susceptibility to propaganda. Inexperience and immaturity in an audience and prestige on the part of a speaker constitute in themselves an appropriate setting for the operation of suggestion. Ignorance, or at least lack of organized knowledge on a particular topic, further increases the probability of ready acceptance. We may conclude, therefore, that without recourse to any dubious methods of indoctrination, children are already sufficiently suggestible by reason of their inexperience and lack of knowledge, reinforced by the superior position and reputation enjoyed by their elders. It is not surprising that as a rule they rapidly absorb the beliefs and attitudes of those around them, especially when in addition they are subjected to the suggestion of mass media such as cinema, television, wireless, comics, and even advertising, all of which bring subtle influences to bear on children's modes of thinking and acting.

In spite of all this, however, the adoption of attitudes that are the converse of those intended is by no means an uncommon occurrence with children. This negative response is called contrasuggestion and it is typical of certain phases of development. Some children are more prone to it than others and they are said, like Mistress Mary in the nursery rhyme, to be quite contrary. There is, admittedly, in any form of suggestion, and particularly in the case of suggestion of a moral kind, a contrasuggestive element which ought always to be taken into account. Otherwise, what to school boys is 'pi-jaw', or 'pep talks' on temperance or the evils of gambling in the case of adults, will run the risk of defeating their own object. On the whole, mere pious exhortation is less likely to generate contrasuggestion than outright prohibition, and this fact has important implications for the work of the teacher. As a consequence, any kind of correction that is framed in a positive way stands a far greater chance of acceptance than negative injunctions. Human frailty seems to respond to New more readily than to Old Testament morality, and the Sermon on the Mount makes greater allowance for man's natural perversity than the Mosaic law of Mount Sinai.

In some circumstances it is possible to counteract this contrasuggestive tendency in human nature by forbidding in advance a certain line of action which those concerned may never have contemplated. A classic example of conveying suggestion by prohibition is to be found in Mark Antony's famous burial speech in Shakespeare's *Julius Caesar*. In this, Antony, while all the time disclaiming any power of oratory or intention of sedition, subtly implants in the minds of the citizens of Rome the idea of revolting against the conspirators:

> . . . let me not stir you up
> To such a sudden flood of mutiny . . .
> For I have neither wit, nor words, nor worth,
> Action, nor utterance, nor power of speech,
> To stir men's blood . . .
> . . . But were I Brutus,
> And Brutus Antony, there were an Antony
> Would ruffle up your spirits, and put a tongue
> In every wound of Caesar, that should move
> The stones of Rome to rise and mutiny.

The very act of forbidding only serves to call the prohibited idea more forcibly to their attention and insinuates a compelling urge to realize it in action. Similarly, the well-known contrariness of children can sometimes be manipulated by a resourceful teacher to produce a desired result. On the other hand, this procedure, by appealing to the disruptive elements in human nature, tends to place children in the painful dilemma of attempting simultaneously both to repress and to carry out the same activity. Consequently, it is seldom to be recommended for use in the classroom.

Much was made at one time by Emile Coué (1857–1926) of the importance of auto-suggestion, although its relevance for educational practice must now be considered doubtful. The therapeutic formula exhibited on the walls of his clinic at Nancy, 'every day, in every way, I am getting better and better', is still familiar to a large number of people. Auto-suggestion of the spontaneous kind is doubtless common enough in the ordinary incidents of childhood. Let us suppose a child falls and 'hurts' himself. In an ambivalent situation of this kind the child's reaction may quite well be to pick himself up and go on playing rather than to believe himself hurt and burst into tears. Spontaneous auto-suggestion is also reinforced by parental attitudes. The calm mother who pats the sore part and proclaims it better checks the impulse to cry, whereas the anxious mother who shows alarm simply encourages the flow of tears. It is probable that the educational implications of deliberate auto-suggestion are rather more important. We all know of the school-boy who, by concentrating immediately before sleep on a mathematical problem whose answer has persistently eluded him, wakes up to find it 'miraculously' solved for him. Coué, however, had a more serious approach than this. He was concerned to develop an elaborate technique for inducing deliberate auto-suggestion, which involved a special concentrated though effortless attention that he called 'contention'. Even so, the only obvious relevance of this for educational purposes is the possibility of its voluntary use by the pupil to overcome undesirable habits, e.g., nail-biting. A favourite maxim with Coué was that whatever suggestion has caused it can cure. On the other hand, he would not limit the curative powers of suggestion merely to phenomena induced in this way.

We may conclude that auto-suggestion is of comparatively rare occurrence in the average pupil, and that for practical purposes the teacher need concern himself only with hetero-suggestion. The influence that he can expect to exert through this medium is, however, by no means unlimited, and so there is no point in entertaining exaggerated doubts about the propriety of using it. Certainly, so far as overt action is concerned, it is a well-established fact that suggestion can do no more than set in motion tendencies that are already there. Even in the hypnotic state the subject cannot be induced to perform actions that run counter to the whole trend of his personality. Admittedly, beliefs are more susceptible than action to the influence of suggestion, and it is not generally very difficult to inculcate in the receptive minds of children such undesirable attitudes as prejudice and intolerance. The very word 'suggestive' itself has all sorts of unpleasant connotations. Yet, as St. Paul assured Titus, unto the pure all things are pure. Fundamentally the wish is very often father to the thought and external influences have little to do with the matter. Nevertheless, it would be a little disingenuous to imply that, without resorting to the crude methods of the 'brainwasher', the unscrupulous teacher is incapable of the improper use of suggestion in his teaching. Truth may indeed be deliberately distorted by either positive or tacit misrepresentation, known technically as *suggestio falsi* and *suppressio veri*. That is why witnesses in law courts are required to swear to tell the 'whole' truth and 'nothing but' the truth in regard to the evidence they give.

In these days of powerful ideologies the question arises whether it is desirable to expose pupils to the influence of teachers of known extremist views. This is in many ways a difficult question to answer. As a teaching method suggestion operates most pervasively in the ethical and aesthetic fields, and so it is in connection with the inculcation of morality and standards of value that the problem is most acute. So far as religious instruction is concerned, one of the advantages of the denominational school is that it can uninhibitedly provide dogmatic teaching. In county schools the modern safeguard of the agreed syllabus, although probably less unsatisfactory than was at one time thought, is still generally regarded as an inadequate substitute for denominational teaching. Its main disadvantage is that in adhering to it the conscientious teacher may have to restrain a perfectly legitimate enthusiasm. Nowadays, it is true, the other extreme is perhaps more likely, namely lack of enthusiasm rather than fervour. This fact, however, does not afford any grounds for complacency, for in many respects indifference is even more regrettable than excess of zeal. If the dominant method of conveying religious beliefs is through the medium of suggestion, the absence of enthusiasm must inevitably render such teaching largely ineffectual. However technically competent may be the presentation of the subject-matter, indifference in the teacher can only nullify its influence for good. On the other hand, simulated enthusiasm is unlikely to succeed, since children are expert at detecting sham.

In view of children's reaction against too blatant moralizing, the inculcation of qualities such as self-control, kindliness, truthfulness and the like, also calls for highly judicious use of suggestion on the teacher's part. In the aesthetic field, too, even where a good model is shown to them, children are apt to be alienated by dogmatic statements of the reasons for appreciating its artistic merit. Consequently we have little choice but to take the teacher on trust and to rely on his professional integrity not to abuse our faith in his impartiality. It is probably in the political sphere that the greatest danger at present lies. But even there open adherence to a particular ideology may have less harmful effects than is sometimes supposed. The known proselytizer will no doubt arouse a healthy scepticism in his pupils or have his views counteracted by enthusiasts of a different political allegiance. It is otherwise, however, with the man who veils his opinions. Whether his purpose is innocent or malicious, his influence is likely to be far more insidious. Thus the repressed fascist or the crypto-communist can do much more to inhibit the healthy development of democratic attitudes in pupils than the avowed party member. The best defence against insinuating influences of this kind is the open examination of tendentious arguments. *Straight and Crooked Thinking*, by R. H. Thouless, and *Thinking to Some Purpose*, by Susan Stebbing, are the two best-known works in this field. Though they are too advanced for use in schools, there now exist a number of simpler books for school-children along similar lines. In so far as such exercises do little to promote constructive ideas, some people are inclined to regard them, like coaching for intelligence tests, as a waste of precious educational time. Children are, nevertheless, notoriously vulnerable to fallacious reasoning, and the exposure of error may often be as valuable for them as the demonstration of truth.

Misleading suggestion is not confined to the teacher. The pupil's everyday background is frequently responsible for instilling undesirable attitudes that the well-disposed teacher may do his best to neutralize. But it is extremely hard for him to divest words in common use of their emotive overtones, e.g., nigger, pacifist, capitalist, etc. At a less serious level the suggestion of superficial elements, like frogs and snails with the French or kilts and bagpipes with Scotland, though often harmless enough, is on the whole to be discouraged in the classroom. Popular fallacies that distort objective truth are sometimes difficult to dispel, e.g., that lunatics are affected by the moon. Even the accidental form of words can convey a false impression, and children may find it difficult to accept, for instance, that earwigs have no connection with ears or Welsh rabbit with rabbit. Figures are an even graver source of misrepresentation. Statistics, we are told, can be made to prove anything, and this not only for vague abstractions like population trends or the cost-of-living index. In everyday life percentages can be used to inflate gains and ordinary fractions to minimize losses. Eighty per cent passes in an examination may sound more impressive than sixteen out of twenty candidates successful, but on the debit side we may overlook the fact that one-sixth is greater than one-eighth. If the headmaster is guilty of some juggling with figures on speech day, this can no doubt be passed off as a comparatively innocent piece of deception for parental consumption. In the classroom, however, there are relatively harmless forms of suggestion that fall short of professional standards. Among these we may mention the teacher who uses excessive prompting, especially in the presence of a visitor, to secure the desired answers, or the one who places overmuch reliance on artificial mnemonics as an aid to retention on the part of his pupils.

Of the broad educational methods so far considered, suggestion is admittedly a more imperfect instrument for inculcating cold scientific truth than either deductive or inductive reasoning. To concede this does not necessarily give grounds for depreciating its value as a medium of teaching. Even if the ultimate establishment of reason as the pupil's sole guide is the teacher's avowed object, he can hardly afford to ignore so useful a factor as human suggestibility. An important tendency of the human mind is actively to discover reasons for buttressing a partial truth implanted by suggestion. A striking example of this phenomenon is to be found in the operation of post-hypnotic suggestion: as a result of this the subject will often invent quite plausible reasons for performing in the waking state irrational, though harmless, actions suggested to him during hypnosis. Similarly, ideas once implanted in the mind progress imperceptibly by the spontaneous exercise of thought. It is true that the element of rationalization may not always be along desired lines: the pupil may either decry the opinions of others as less well-founded than his own or magnify the validity of his own arguments in the teeth of logical flaws. Even so, the sweet reasonableness of an impartial teacher can do much to influence the development of wholesome attitudes and balanced views. Whilst suggestion normally operates downwards from superiors to subordinates, it may also spread its influence among equals. It can therefore work laterally from pupil to pupil and so reinforce the general effect of the teacher's efforts without further exertion on his part. Indeed, the whole ethos or tone of a school greatly depends on what is accepted as good form by the school community and this in turn derives in the first instance from the dominant ideals of its teaching staff. The suggestion which is embalmed in tradition can be a most valuable influence for good in any educational institution.

The class as a teaching unit is constantly under fire from progressive educationists who stress the importance of individual activities in the classroom. Suggestion is, however, essentially a collective method of instruction and fits in well with accepted school organization. Though pre-eminently an instrument of moral and social education, it also has a distinctive part to play in intellectual education. It is not only in ethical matters that enthusiasm is infectious; a ready response to a new subject of study from a class of pupils is almost always directly due to the personal influence of an eager teacher. A really keen headmaster may even redirect the traditional bias of a school from the classics to mathematics or science, if it suits his purpose. Nevertheless, it is in subjects that most readily admit of inspirational teaching, such as literature, history or music, that the use of suggestion, applied to intellectual instruction, is clearly most appropriate. Appreciation of any kind is only too likely to fall flat unless the teacher is in a position to com-municate it to a reasonably large and homogeneous group of pupils. One of the early advocates of popular education, David Stow (1793–1864), made a great deal of what he called the 'sympathy of numbers'. It still seems true that the most successful teaching of subjects of this kind requires a fusion of individual responses for its maximum effect. By means of suggestion the skilful teacher can give point and direction to the otherwise ephemeral emotional experiences generated by the lyric quality of the poetry lesson or the vivid narrative of the history period. In the oral work that forms a part of all teaching that is not purely factual, sug-gestion comes into play. Accordingly, it would be a mistake to regard suggestibility as merely an irrational failing of childhood and so grant other agencies a monopoly of its use in influencing the young.

Suggestions for Further Reading:

Adams, Sir J., *Exposition and Illustration in Teaching*, Macmillan, 1909.
Baudouin, C., *Suggestion and Autosuggestion*, Allen & Unwin, 1920.
Drever, J., *An Introduction to the Psychology of Education*, Arnold, 1922.
Keatinge, M. W., *Suggestion in Education*, Black, 1911.
Nunn, Sir T. P., *Education: Its Data and First Principles*, Arnold, 1945.
Pinsent, A., *The Principles of Teaching-Method*, Harrap, 1941.

CHAPTER VII

IMITATION AND CREATIVITY
IN CHILDREN

IMITATION in the learner is the psychological correlative of suggestion on the part of the teacher. The bearing of this on educational practice has been somewhat overlooked, and as a result the full significance of imitation as a factor in personal growth has only recently come to be recognized. Yet the social importance of imitation in the development of the mental life of the individual child is difficult to over-estimate, for it serves as the channel through which the experience of one generation is transmitted to the next as a basis for further development. Nowadays much that was formerly ascribed to heredity is seen to be due to imitation, such as the tricks of gesture and speech in certain families, and it is no doubt on that account that the real function of this psychological trait remained masked for so long. Children are, admittedly, particularly susceptible to the imitative tendency, but we misunderstand its true nature if we are inclined to think of it as in any sense a mark of immaturity. On the contrary, imitation is a universal propensity shared by old and young alike, on which morality itself and the whole social fabric ultimately depends. We may certainly deplore narrow plagiarism in art or literature and yet agree that in a broad sense the gains of one can, through the agency of imitation, become the possession of all without detriment to the originator. Few of us are immune to the prevailing ideas of our time and we tend quite unconsciously to absorb the thoughts and feelings of those around us. At the same time we make them our own and thus we are not merely imitative. No doubt the strongest educational influence of the example of others is to be found in the creation of appropriate attitudes, but by overtly copying the activities of other people children may make great progress in the acquirement of physical skills.

In effect, imitation is the executive or conative aspect of suggestion, and very often it is sufficient simply to watch someone else engaged on a novel task for the observer to experience a strong urge to do likewise. The tendency for ideas to act themselves out in what is called ideomotor action is now an accepted commonplace of educational psychology. The advantage of such action is that it appears to the imitator as self-initiated. To a child, accordingly, it is likely to afford much greater satisfaction than similar action carried out merely on the instruction of some external authority. The imitation of other people's activities not only stimulates children to undertake the kind of task they could in any case have accomplished on their own initiative; it also brings home to them what they could not accomplish without having a model or pattern to follow. Through copying others they will become aware of their own capacity for achievement in directions which they might otherwise consider beyond their powers. Even quite slavish imitation may have this effect, although intelligent appreciation of the processes involved is always to be preferred. It is important, nevertheless, to realize that in imitation the pupil's innate ability to perform independently the same general level of activity effectively conditions the measure of his success. We delude ourselves if we fondly hope to create ability that is not already potentially there. The most that can reasonably be expected of imitation is that it may help to develop and improve an existing potential. In consequence, Dewey and others have laid down as a sound educational principle that, generally speaking, no activity should be originated in the pupil purely by imitation. A wiser course, they feel, is to wait for the initiative to come from him, and only then to supply him with an appropriate model or copy to assist him in realizing more fully his own conceptions.

As a means of learning, imitation suffers from the limitation that unless in actual execution the pupil succeeds in getting away from his model, he will remain over-dependent and so fail to develop the requisite personal autonomy. This is a common failing in the construction of many school textbooks. They may provide the learner with excellent examples of rules or models, and yet in the accompanying exercises show little imagination in allowing for possible deviations from the set pattern. As a result pupils will tend to have a purely mechanical knowledge of the rule or proposition discussed and little adaptability in applying it to fresh situations. For educational purposes we must be careful to differentiate between two kinds of imitation. The young child very often acts, in the rather hackneyed words of Wordsworth,

> As if his whole vocation
> Were endless imitation.
> (*Ode on Intimations of Immortality*)

This is the spontaneous imitation, which Sir Percy Nunn terms 'mimesis', that dominates the dramatic play of children when they imitate the doings of their elders directly and not as a means to an ulterior end. The activity itself is intrinsically attractive to the child, and in this kind of imitation ideas are not necessarily involved at all. It is clear, nevertheless, that a great part of the groundwork of subsequent intellectual and emotional development is in fact derived from unconscious imitation of the speech and actions of parents. As is the case with auto-suggestion, there is also a deliberate kind of imitation which has a greater educational significance and which does necessarily involve an ideational element. In this instance the child starts off with the idea of a certain end to be attained, and it is for the sake of this end, rather than for its own sake, that his activity is carried on.

In the case of deliberate imitation, the end, though ulterior in one sense, may be more or less direct. The boy who is bent on carving a model aeroplane out of wood may very well lay most stress on faithful reproduction of the pattern. On the other hand, the end itself is often indirect. In constructing a rough-and-ready sledge, a boy is more likely to be interested in increased speed of movement than in great accuracy of representation. We need not make too much of this distinction, for in any case the educational consequences are likely to be of value. Deliberate imitation, whether the end be direct or indirect, has the effect of demanding from the pupil a much closer attention to detail than would be required for mere recognition of the particular subject-matter. A further beneficial effect that it may have is to contribute to the general raising of standards of achievement within a group by arousing emulation among the different members of a class. We may think of imitation as mainly concerned with what is immediately perceived, and no doubt this is generally its most effective mode. But we should not overlook the importance of the ideational imitation stimulated by reading books. In this way children are introduced to a wider and more representative society than they can hope to meet in everyday life. This is particularly valuable during adolescence, when both literature and history provide a rich garner of models which young people should be encouraged to seek out for themselves with relatively little guidance from parents and teachers.

The social importance of the imitative tendency in the community at large is therefore highly significant. 'Playing the game' in school, convention in the wider society outside, even professional etiquette are all ultimately based upon it.

The doctor's bedside manner, the solicitor's inscrutability, the clergyman's cordiality, the schoolmaster's preciseness are all in their way manifestations of the tendency in operation. There may, of course, be an element of mumbo-jumbo in professional codes that merely serves to perpetuate outmoded practices, and this is doubtless to be deprecated. But on the whole the propensity to imitate is constructive and should be fostered. At all events it is so pervasive that a discerning teacher will constantly be on his guard to be an example to his pupils. This does not mean that he should hold himself up as a conscious model for imitation; except when expressly demonstrating a specific technique, he is well advised to avoid exposing himself unnecessarily. Even in the definite inculcation of skills, however, there are some teachers who hesitate to impose their personal authority through fear of inhibiting the creative impulse in their pupils. Such diffidence is generally misguided. We may admit that, given the requisite instruments and appropriate materials, children unaided can no doubt acquire a measure of skill in using them. It is none the less probable that the result will be achieved only at the expense of uneconomic methods of approach, faulty technique and a good deal of discouragement in the process.

To depreciate imitation as liable to stifle individuality is a mistaken view. Even the close copying of a model leaves a surprising amount of scope for individual variation. It has been found, for instance, that the copybook writing of school-children can display a wide variety of personal characteristics. Now, if this is the case with a more or less mechanical task, the possibilities for developing through imitation an original technique in complex activities must obviously be infinitely greater. In literature or art, for instance, Shakespeare borrowed freely from Holinshed without prejudice to his own genius, and Rossetti triumphantly perfected an individualistic style of painting through deliberate imitation of the pre-Raphaelite Italian artists.

Even in the history of education, all the great educators of the Renaissance are known to have modelled themselves on Quintilian without detracting from the intellectual brilliance of a great age. The fact is that although imitation and creativity are often set in opposition, there is no very clearly marked antithesis between them. On the other hand, it may well be that the exaggerated respect nowadays accorded to the so-called 'creativeness' of children will come to be regarded by posterity as a peculiar aberration of our time. It is not long since anything in the nature of creative power was solemnly attributed to God alone. Now, however, the term 'creative' is freely applied not only to the higher activities of men of genius but even to the everyday products of children. It is popularly supposed, despite clear evidence to the contrary, that educationally subnormal children are endowed with special compensatory 'creative' powers in drawing and handwork. As a rule this is quite untrue.

Certainly it is chiefly in the aesthetic sphere of art, craft and composition that originality is actively encouraged in children. In the more formal exercises of spelling, grammar and punctuation, individual eccentricity, once tolerated, is now not only frowned upon but conformity is even considered a desirable quality. The fashion of attributing to children creative activity probably originated with Froebel, who held mystic views on the unity in God of all things, including human nature, which he saw as partly universal (hence Godlike), partly individual, partly diverse. Admittedly, only one aspect of man's triune nature (the 'universal' element) links him directly with God, but we may assume that his oneness with the Creator invests man with some part in the divine attribute of creativity. As it happened, this sentimental point of view was speedily superseded by the Darwinian hypothesis of the adaptation of the organism to its natural environment. Nevertheless, in so far as such adaptation posited on occasion a capacity to reconstruct the environment, the evolutionary doctrine continued to imply a creative element on the part of the organism. Hence there remained a tendency for writers who, like Sir Percy Nunn, came under the influence of biological naturalism to equate creative capacity with such concepts as growth, adaptation and even psychic activity in general. Other writers who, like W. H. Kilpatrick, have been influenced by the philosophic doctrine of pragmatism, are inclined to go further still and to see even mechanical processes as creative. For them the learning process, for instance, is regarded not as the acquisition of what already exists but as an activity creative of its own subject-matter. The child is a potential creator of values.

On the other hand, the obvious existence of an already established culture is clearly undeniable, and this kind of reasoning places pragmatists in an awkward dilemma. To meet the difficulty Kilpatrick has recourse to postulating two sorts of creativity. What he calls 'psychological' creation is concerned merely with the manipulation of accepted ideas. In the case of 'sociological' creation, however, these are thrown into fresh combinations in such a way as to constitute an addition to the group culture. If we take the existence of language as an example, the acquisition of linguistic facility by the individual will involve only psychological creation, whereas the composition of lyric poetry, even by a mute inglorious Milton, will entail some degree of sociological creation. The pragmatist would assert that every fresh situation with which we are faced is sufficiently novel to call for some creative act to meet it, even though he might not deny that the element of uniqueness in any given situation can at best only be relative. Unless we are able to relate the new situation to some previous experience in accordance with the Herbartian principle of apperception, clearly it must remain wholly unintelligible to us. Even so, only what Kilpatrick calls sociological creation, as adding something of value to the cultural inheritance of the race, can ever be considered creative in the true sense of the word. If this be our criterion it is idle to look for such contributions from other than a minority of exceptional minds.

It should not be supposed, however, that even Dewey himself goes so far as to regard children's whims as altogether sacrosanct. He was too much of a realist to advocate abandoning pupils to their own devices in the fond belief that something valuable and original would result from their activities, unless these clearly formed part of a planned and consciously directed purpose. In spite of this, there can be little doubt that the cumulative effect of the continued attribution of creativeness to human activity has been to encourage the assumption that man is naturally endowed with some specific mental capacity, which for convenience we may call creative ability. Unfortunately, the precise nature of this aptitude is by no means clearly defined, and in the absence of certainty three possibilities— none of them really satisfactory—suggest themselves for consideration. The first possibility is that there is a 'faculty' of creativeness in man's psychological make-up. Against this it may be said at once that there are no better grounds for postulating a faculty of this kind than (say) a faculty of memory or reasoning such as are now discredited in current psychological thought. Slightly more hopeful is the possibility of the existence of a creativity 'factor', analogous to the verbal (v) or spatial (k) factors that are generally regarded as constituent traits in human ability. The objection to this hypothesis is that so far no such factor has been isolated by factorial analysis. The third possibility, implied in certain works on child art, is that of a creative 'instinct'. The usual psychological classifications of man's instinctive equipment do not, however, make provision for the inclusion of any such instinct; and although William McDougall does allow for a constructive instinct, it appears to be particularly concerned with house-building and similar co-operative enterprises.

We are, nevertheless, probably quite justified in assuming in children the existence of some kind of creative urge, though it may well be independent of any specific purposes or materials. It seems possible that creativeness in this sense is not a simple innate power at all, but rather a somewhat complex stage in mental development which may express itself in a number of diverse forms—literary, scientific, aesthetic, etc. Furthermore, from the investigations of anthropologists such as Margaret Mead in New Guinea, it would seem to be culturally conditioned rather than inborn. Yet so distrustful of authoritarian influences on children's creativeness was the great Viennese exponent of child art, Franz Cisek, that he declared outright that it would be better for them to be brought up on a desert island far from artistic examples of any kind. This pronouncement need not be taken at its face value, however, for when Margaret Mead provided primitive children with the requisite opportunities for creative and imaginative activity she failed to find any work produced that could be called art. The divergence of opinion is probably to be explained by the fact that, as a result of our failure to identify all the various influences to which the child is inevitably exposed, we are sometimes led to attribute to him the possession of more clearly marked innate creative powers than can be strictly justified.

On the other hand, we do well to recognize that it is in response to just such intangible influences, quite as much as spontaneously, that a child produces any creative work. To some extent, therefore, even the most original artist or writer cannot but be circumscribed by the conventions of his age and country. Accordingly, what we have to determine in education is whether the pupil should be left to encounter these influences casually, or whether we are justified in so manipulating the aesthetic elements in his cultural environment as to make his experience of them most likely to be fruitful. It would be vain to imagine that in any event teachers can ever hope to avoid influencing the aesthetic development of their pupils entirely. At most they can only be alive to the danger that their influence, if consciously exerted, may restrict and stereotype, instead of liberating and extending, the range of children's creative activities. In the course of his investigations into the nature of creative activity, Victor Lowenfeld discovered clear evidence that early value judgments and intentions tended all too readily to become crystallized later into purely formal, inflexible and mechanical representations. We must therefore discourage undue precociousness in creative expression, while at the same time endeavouring to maintain and develop the pupil's freedom in this field. To this end the gradual encouragement of conscious intelligent control, in place of the uncertain and haphazard control of external agencies, seems highly desirable even at the risk of a small loss in spontaneity.

Conscious intelligent control, although perhaps most readily apparent in the intellectual effort involved in a scientific discovery, is in fact characteristic of the higher forms of creative activity as practised by the great masters in any aesthetic medium. We may agree with Ben Jonson that a good poet is made as well as born, and assume that in any sphere truly creative work requires a full and complete mastery of the technique of the medium employed. Obviously this cannot be acquired without a certain degree of intellectual development. If, indeed, we may regard a scientific discovery as an act of the creative imagination no less than creations in literature, art or music, we can at once appreciate the fallacy of overestimating the creative ability of children. On this basis it would hardly be more reasonable to suppose children capable of making a significant contribution in art or literature, without first mastering its special technique, than to expect from an amateur, untrained in science or mathematics, an important advance in physics or astronomy. It is true certainly that the actual

·suggestion which stimulates a creative artist to activity is very often an idea of no great complexity. Sometimes even the pattern on which this idea is evolved is a design of comparative simplicity. Nevertheless, this does not alter the fact that the composition of a real work of art demands an intensity of effort which is far removed from the spontaneous productions of children. It is not suggested that the products of 'creative writing' in the classroom are not valuable in their own way, but this value is strictly relative.

In the light of these considerations we must decide on the kind of educational treatment that would seem most judicious for fostering true creativity. As we have seen, there are extremists who, for fear of inhibiting the pupil's creative powers, deprecate any suggestion by the teacher, much less active interference, in the child's activities or occupations. We need not take this view too seriously. Even Dewey, while postulating freedom of expression in action as a necessary condition of growth, still regarded proper guidance of that expression as equally essential. In considering art and education he was ready to concede the teacher's right to make helpful suggestions, on the ground that the theory of *laissez-faire*, if carried to its logical conclusion, must exclude the use both of artificial material and of such appliances as are the product of the skill of others. Clearly he is in agreement with Sir Percy Nunn that, in the aesthetic field at least, the teacher is entitled to put his superior knowledge and experience into the common stock from which each of his pupils may draw requisite inspiration. The precise value of such experience will necessarily depend upon its sufficiency in certain specific qualities. In this particular context the most important are first-hand acquaintance with appropriate materials, mastery of varied techniques and possession of a rich repertory of activities. The good teacher, moreover, does not stand still; in the sphere of creativity above all he owes it to his pupils to go on acquainting himself with fresh activities and with new materials as they become available. Fertility of invention is a great asset here. Otherwise, in order to satisfy the insatiable demands of his pupils the teacher will find himself obliged to be for ever borrowing novel designs from every conceivable source. For their benefit also he should be ever ready to go out of his way to obtain the widest possible range of tools and appliances as an aid to creative work.

Undoubtedly the teacher's most important task, however, is to maintain, if he possibly can, his own productiveness. In the humdrum circumstances of everyday teaching this may not always be easy, but it is the only effective way to utilize his own enthusiasm as a stimulus for evoking whatever creative capacity his pupils may possess. Though this may seem most clearly applicable in the case of art and music, it is scarcely less true of literature. It is no bad thing for the English teacher to try his hand from time to time at writing verse or essays. Even the teacher of science is more likely to conjure up in his pupil's mind what Whitehead calls the vision of greatness if he himself continues to be an original experimenter, however modest, in some branch of his subject. There is one respect, however, in which the analogy between inventiveness in scientific discovery and creativeness in the realm of pure fantasy no longer holds good, namely the question of verification. However boldly conceived a scientific theory may be, it can still ultimately be verified, whereas a truly artistic product must always embody an element of uniqueness which is not susceptible of categorization.

This distinction presents us with a very real difficulty. A main obstacle in the way of prescribing generally agreed educational treatment in the aesthetic field is the sad lack of unanimity as to what exactly constitutes art. From the objective point of view a work of art is compounded of an original idea, an appropriate design and a suitably developed technique. Design and technique are no doubt open to criticism by more or less accepted standards, but the whole

defies analysis by any definitive yardstick. From the subjective point of view, art production may or may not be
normally regarded as an accurate representation of external
objects. For the young child, however, it is simply an
expression of feeling, and the teacher must recognize that
very often the pupil is impelled, through the medium of
drawing or painting, just to give outward expression to his
own inner thoughts. In such circumstances, therefore, it is
vain to apply accepted standards of value. If we may adopt
Kilpatrick's distinction, it can be readily conceded that the
products of child art may in themselves have real psychological worth and should be actively encouraged by the
teacher. On the other hand, we should not lose sight of the
fact that without symmetry of design and mastery of technique such products must always be sociologically valueless.
It is not enough merely to encourage the urge to expression;
the teacher must endeavour also to stimulate a sense of
design and foster skill in acquiring technique. If he per-
severes in this, he may hope at the same time to develop in
the pupil a sound aesthetic judgment.

Although artistic appreciation (as distinct from creation)
belongs more strictly, perhaps, to the sphere of suggestion
than of imitation, it should be said that some pupils prove
quite unresponsive to facilities for artistic creativity. In
their case, at least, there is much need to reinforce active
participation with some positive training in aesthetic discrimination, if their artistic sensibility is to be cultivated at
all. In that most children tend in their creative work to be
uncritically imitative, such training has much to be said for
it in all cases. Once again, however, we come up against the
difficulty of a lack of universally accepted canons of artistic
excellence. All the teacher can do here is to introduce his
pupils to acknowledged masterpieces of art and literature
without excessive comment on the nature of their particular
merit. In the aesthetic field, as elsewhere, there is, further,
the likelihood of encountering passive resistance from

children to any suggestion of the things they ought to cherish. From investigations into children's aesthetic sensibilities, an interesting fact emerges in this connection, namely that there is some evidence for believing that they may be less resentful of suggestions about what they ought to reject. We might, therefore, find it a more profitable approach to bring our pupils to recognize the tawdry and the trashy in art, so that eventually they may learn to appreciate the genuine by despising the spurious. In a sense this kind of exercise bears some similarity to the process of detecting fallacious reasoning, except that its subject-matter admits of no final certainty and demands accordingly all the more careful handling.

Suggestions for Further Reading:

Kennedy-Fraser, D., *The Psychology of Education*, Methuen, 1923.
Kilpatrick, W. H., *Remaking the Curriculum*, Newson, 1936.
Lowenfeld, V., *Creative and Mental Growth*, Macmillan, 1952.
Mainwaring, J., *Psychology in the Classroom*, U.L.P., 1956.
Nunn, Sir T. P., *Education: Its Data and First Principles*, Arnold, 1945.
Viola, W., *Child Art*, U.L.P., 1952.

CHAPTER VIII

INTEGRATING THE CURRICULUM

In these days we hear much talk of 'subject-mindedness' in pupils, and certainly the current vogue of early specialization is apt to result in undue isolation of subject-matter in water-tight compartments of the mind. As an antidote to this, Herbart deliberately developed his doctrine of instruction, though using this term in a somewhat special sense. He believed that, when rightly effected, instruction through knowledge creates interest and contributes also to virtue or morality. To be 'educative', instruction should, however, satisfy two criteria: it must neither lack seriousness of purpose nor must it remain in isolation in the pupil's mind. This would no doubt rule out a good deal of instruction of the documentary kind, which is often largely recreational in intention, and it would reject over-specialization out of hand. For Herbart the primary purpose of all instruction was to organize the pupil's ideas in accordance with the educator's own aim. The teacher might do this directly either by supplying the ideas himself or by utilizing the pupil's personal experience for the purpose; or he might do it indirectly by rectifying misconceptions that already existed in the pupil's mind. The direct procedure Herbart regarded as synthetic, and the indirect procedure as analytic, instruction. For practical purposes the distinguishing feature between one and the other was whether the teacher is responsible, or not, for determining in the first instance the particular sequence of ideas in the pupil's mind.

Where synthetic instruction is concerned, the teacher can implant these ideas immediately by means of what Herbart calls description; or else all he need do is to raise to consciousness latent apperception masses. In analytic instruction his task is rather more complex, for here he has to rearrange ideas already derived from previous experience though in a form or order which conflicts with his preconceived plan. The laboriousness of this was succinctly stated long ago by George Snell (1649): 'It is more than a threefold work to unteach that which is wrong and to teach the contrary' (*The Right Teaching of Useful Knowledge*). However that may be, to some it may appear largely a matter of chance whether such previous experience happens to be, from the teacher's point of view, educative or miseducative. For them a more satisfactory basis for differentiating instruction would simply be that the experience utilized is vicarious (i.e., supplied by the teacher) or authentic (i.e., the pupil's own), whether or not this stands in need of correction. At all events, Herbart himself speaks of instruction of the descriptive kind as 'purely presentative' and of instruction based on undoctored authentic experience as 'truly synthetic'. His separate classification, under the head of 'analytic', of instruction involving refined experience, appeared even to one of his own followers, Wilhelm Rein, as somewhat arbitrary. Rein personally preferred to take the content of the new subject-matter as a basis for classifying instruction and he in turn speaks merely of 'narrative' and 'developmental' presentation.

The majority of practical teachers, nevertheless, would probably agree that a threefold classification really corresponds better with the facts. Often enough the pupil's everyday experience may already have supplied the necessary data and the teacher need only integrate the ideas into a desired unity of knowledge by 'truly synthetic' instruction. At other times, even though the pupil may have at his disposal some of the requisite data, the teacher will require to furnish supplementary matter by means of 'purely pre-sentative' instruction. In other instances, the data when first encountered may have been so misleading that the teacher must set about clearing up misconceptions through 'analytic' instruction. The so-called 'facts of life' may serve as a simple example of what is implied in all this. Country children from ordinary observation may have a fair notion of mating and parturition among animals, and little is required in extending such knowledge to human beings. City children, on the other hand, may well need a good deal more 'background' before information of this kind can be properly understood. Excessively sheltered children, who have been brought up on stories of storks or doctors' little black bags, may even have to be 'let down gently' before the topic can be broached at all. 'Unlearning' is most serious where a technique, particularly a neuro-muscular skill, is involved. The faulty performance may have to be stripped down and begun again from scratch. A pupil who has learned to hold his pen wrongly, or one who has picked up a defective style in swimming, will probably require quite intensive coaching before getting rid of his slovenly habits. With more purely factual matter less drastic measures will usually suffice, unless flagrantly bad teaching has aggravated the position. In this respect outmoded methods in arith-metic are the most likely cause of difficulties. As a rule, all that is called for is a slight readjustment of erroneous impressions gathered by the pupil from everyday experi-ence, generally as a result of his faulty powers of analysis. He very often tends to assume the relations perceived between two characters as invariable, and in such a case the appropriate corrective is merely the idea of relativity. Con-stant observation of a connection between size and weight, for example, may well lead the child to believe that, irrespec-tive of material, a larger object will invariably be heavier than a smaller one. In the ordinary way it should not prove unduly difficult to clear up simple misconceptions of this kind.

Herbart's object in introducing such careful classification was to guard against merely casual instruction. The type of instruction which he calls purely presentative frankly recognizes the need for 'telling' in much of the routine work of teaching. This approach is nowadays rather suspect in progressive circles, but Herbart himself, while not blind to its shortcomings, had no doubt that skill in narration and description was by far the surest means of securing interest. Even today instruction of this kind plays a predominant part at the primary level in the teaching of literature, history and descriptive geography. A main disadvantage is that, if too extensively employed, it may well leave the bulk of the work to the teacher instead of the pupils. As the most appropriate subject-matter for the truly synthetic type of instruction, Herbart instances mathematics, but he would include also any studies conducing to the pupil's initiation into the cultural achievements of the race, e.g. social studies, aesthetics, etc. In a wider setting the ordinary business of eliciting facts from a class and organizing these for final presentation in oral or written form may be cited as a proper occasion for its use. The analytic type of instruction, on the other hand, is to be employed chiefly to correct and systematize the inchoate teachings of everyday experience rather than as serving an end in itself. Its function is thus in a sense therapeutic, and its purpose is mainly to prepare the way for further synthesis somewhat after the manner of Socrates. The danger inherent in the analytic approach is, however, that the teaching may so easily degenerate into mere questioning and be lacking in constructive value.

In Herbart's view it is only by constant regulation of the kind of instruction given that a proper seriousness of purpose can be attained. In general we may go so far as to agree with him that teaching procedure should be neither purely analytic nor purely synthetic but a judicious blend of each. Writing on some general principles, Lord James of Rusholme suggests three kinds of justification for including any subject in the school curriculum (*An Essay on the Content of Education*). They are that it should convey information essential to the business of living, that it should inculcate valuable skills, and that it should contribute to the spiritual development of the individual. Every good lesson should no doubt also contain an element of each of these attributes; yet unless the teacher appropriately varies his technique to suit the particular ingredient, a confusion of purposes may well result. A poetry lesson, such as *The Burial of Sir John Moore*, by Charles Wolfe, or *The Charge of the Light Brigade*, by Lord Tennyson, is doubtless primarily intended to foster literary appreciation, but it may be used as material for extending the pupils' knowledge of history or even for developing their powers of diction. In Herbart's terminology, the instruction will thus be successively truly synthetic, purely presentative and, possibly, analytic. The important point is that if the teacher, in such a lesson, should fail to adapt his style of teaching to each distinctive aspect, none of his purposes may be achieved.

While setting great store by relevant and operative ideas, Herbart regarded disconnected facts as valueless. Nevertheless, he admits that his treatment of the different types of instruction, as applied to the various fields of human interests, was not sufficiently detailed to deal with the curriculum as a whole. It was, therefore, largely left to his followers to suggest remedies to counteract the lack of integration that inevitably characterizes much of the instruction given in schools. The two expedients they proposed were based on the principles of co-ordination and of subordination respectively. Correlation of studies, as they called the first, was designed to link together facts, processes and subjects that have a mutual bearing on one another. The difficulty here was that teachers tended to discover trivial and artificial links between subjects that were really quite disparate. There were jibes, for instance, about linking Latin on to statics and co-ordinating theology with higher mathematics. As an antidote to this, the second expedient, which they called concentration of studies, was put forward as a more drastic alternative. Instead of attempting the intercorrelation of school subjects of equal standing, this represented rather an endeavour to correlate these round a core of leading facts or skills. The most celebrated experiment of this kind was the so-called 'culture epoch theory', in which certain periods of history, both religious and secular, were taken as the centre round which the teaching of all else was to revolve. This principle was found to have the disadvantage of easily degenerating into pedantry in the hands of inexpert practitioners.

As a corrective to mental isolation co-ordination seeks to unify various aspects of school subjects which might otherwise be presented entirely independently. It is a pedagogic device designed to enable the pupil to organize his knowledge more efficiently. This it does in two ways: by bridging over the boundaries of conventional school subjects, and by preventing needless overlapping. Thus it helps both to avoid gaps in teaching and to guard against the same topic being presented all over again by another teacher or even by the same teacher in a different kind of lesson. The basic idea is that if geography is required to explain a certain aspect of history or physics a feature of geography, the historian temporarily turns geographer, the geographer becomes a physicist, and so on. Though we may concede that the rigid segregation of school subjects has the great advantage of systematizing the subject-matter, we do well to recognize that for the pupil it has three serious drawbacks. It tends, firstly, to divorce school work from life, so that current affairs are not seen as a part of history or local studies as connected with geography. Secondly, it introduces an unfortunate dichotomy between theory and practice, so that composition is associated with formal essay-writing but not with the natural expression of thoughts in a private letter. Thirdly, it puts blinkers on ideas as a source of illumination in separate disciplines, so that analysis is a quite different mental operation for the grammarian and the chemist.

Notwithstanding all this, Dewey is opposed to any form of artificial correlation. To produce the desired effect he would rely entirely on the community and continuity of subject-matter rather than on devices employed by the teacher. For him it suffices that the school be related to life for all studies to be automatically correlated. We may think, however, that this somewhat artless view fails to take sufficient account of the deep-seated tendency of the human mind to compartmentalize its activities. The problem confronting the teacher is how to achieve a certain technical efficiency without also encouraging mental rigidity. To some extent his pupil has to be turned into a specialist without at the same time becoming a pedant. He must, for instance, learn to apply grammatical rules to the correction of speech and yet avoid being a purist in ordinary conversation. If we allow the reaction against the inviolability of school subjects to go too far, we simply substitute anarchy for tyranny. Co-ordination is a common-sense attempt to break down barriers between segregated domains of knowledge without seeking to abolish their separate title. Every branch of study is concurrently taught with due emphasis not only on the connections between each one but on the essential equality of the individual subjects.

With the principle of subordination, on the other hand, these interconnections between co-ordinate studies tend to be replaced by coherence on a central theme of a number of subordinate subjects. The Herbartians thus used the term concentration in substantially its ordinary meaning of focusing the mind on a specific area of thought. By directing attention to a narrower range of thinking they hoped to prevent the dissipation of mental energy on a multiplicity of ideas. The underlying theory was to give point and direction to study by setting permanently at the centre of the curriculum a single subject, and concentrating round this core all the rest. While the classics reigned supreme, the only history and geography normally taught in grammar schools was of the kind that would throw light on the central subject of instruction, i.e. ancient history and geography of the Mediterranean. With the decay of the classics under the influence of naturalism, the Herbartians in Germany attempted to substitute some form of history as the core of the curriculum. However, as a result of the rise of other modern studies, strong claims were staked in this country in the course of the last century for science and English as central subjects. Herbert Spencer's advocacy of science in this role (1859) is well known:

> We conclude, then, that for discipline, as well as for guidance, science is of chiefest value. . . . Whether for intellectual, moral, or religious training, the study of surrounding phenomena is immensely superior to the study of grammars and lexicons (*What Knowledge is of Most Worth?*).

An equally cogent plea for English in this capacity was made thirty years later (1890) by S. S. Laurie:

> Whether we regard the discipline of intellect, the substance of morality and wisdom, or the growth of the distinctively spiritual life, language . . . is, and must always be, the supreme subject in the education of a human being, the centre round which all other educational agencies ought to range themselves in due subordination. In conclusion, when I say that language is the supreme subject in all education, I mean the vernacular language (*Language and Linguistic Method in the School*).

Difficult though it is to adjudicate between these conflicting claims, it is even more difficult to escape the conclusion that under modern conditions the principle of subordination presents far greater practical objections than that of co-ordination, whatever subject be selected as the integrative core. Three immediate disadvantages may be mentioned. In the first place, the order of lessons in all but the pivotal subject is liable to be dislocated, and the subordinate subjects are inevitably thrown out of gear. As a result, systematic teaching becomes well-nigh impossible and we cannot seriously imagine a satisfactory course of chemistry, for instance, that is primarily based on history. Secondly, whatever does not happen to fit in conveniently with the syllabus of the central subject may well have to be omitted by the teacher when dealing with the subordinate subjects. Arbitrary curtailment of this kind is hardly likely to encourage the developing interests of the pupils. Finally, however varied a teacher's approach may be, too much concentration on a core subject can very easily lead to a feeling of surfeit in the learners. Although himself disposed to attach special significance to geography and history and to science in the course of study, Dewey is hostile also to the idea of concentration. Speaking of educational values, he states unequivocally: 'We cannot establish a hierarchy of values among studies' (*Democracy and Education*).

What the Herbartians called concentration must not be confused with the employment of what is sometimes known as the concentric method. In its fullest application this embraces a group of subjects which are pursued throughout the whole course of study, in circles of ever-widening sweep to accord with the pupil's mental development. The classic example is the concentric type of curriculum advocated in *The Great Didactic* of J. A. Comenius, in which each individual subject is to be begun in the nursery and continued through the school, though specifically adapted to the needs of infancy, boyhood and adolescence. For Comenius, language will thus comprise speech, study of the vernacular, foreign tongues, and science will consist of object lessons, then nature study, followed by natural philosophy. Nowadays, however, we do not subscribe to the view that every subject can be appropriately introduced at the kindergarten level or profitably taught to every pupil throughout his school career. We may well feel that some subjects are better postponed to a later stage, or that others should be dropped long before the end of the secondary course. As applied to particular subjects in the curriculum, the concentric method of treatment is opposed to the division of subject-matter into undifferentiated sections for retailing to the learners. Such an approach clearly is better adapted to the teaching of some subjects than others, and it has proved most successful with history, geography and science.

Textbooks constructed on the concentric principle very often cover the same general ground throughout, e.g., a period in history or a region in geography, but at each successive stage some effort is made to widen systematically the circle of information. In dealing with a particular period of history, for instance, we may adopt a mainly biographical approach in the first cycle, treat events in the second, and stress causes in the third. Or in studying a region in geography, we may perhaps begin with a description of the inhabitants, come back to a treatment of industries and products, and end up with a consideration of physical features and climate. Thus, although a comprehensive picture of (say) Stuart England or the southern continents may not immediately emerge, it is contended that this approach has a positive advantage over full treatment of particular topics at one stage. There is obviously less danger of total omission from a given pupil's mental equipment of any important aspect of the syllabus. Quite apart from any psychological considerations that may be involved, a prolonged period of absence from school may result in an unfortunate gap in the pupil's knowledge if, for instance, we attempt to deal with all aspects of the Commonwealth period, or of South Africa, in a single cycle. Nevertheless, we would expect the main justification of a concentric approach to learning to reside in its adaptability to mental growth; and in this respect one of the more fruitful proposals has been the so-called 'wonder-utility-system' formula originally advanced by Sir Percy Nunn as long ago as 1905. Although designed to apply chiefly to the teaching of mathematics and science, this formula none the less contained possibilities of more general application.

In the development of many cultural traditions Nunn discerned a natural rhythm which began in wonder, proceeded through utility and ended in system. Such a rhythm is perhaps most easily illustrated from developments in science, and Nunn quotes as a typical example the growth of electro-magnetism. Nevertheless, it was his contention that analogous phases could be traced in humanistic subjects, such as the development of history, and even in the aesthetic field in the evolution of art. Even more significant was Nunn's conviction that the reactions of pupils corresponded closely to the natural stages in the historical development of these cultural traditions. In other words, he believed not only that human activities normally follow a certain pattern in their evolution but also that children should be introduced to these activities, once evolved, by recapitulating the stages of development. He concluded, accordingly, that interest in the wonderful is the starting-point for intellectual growth in any branch of study, e.g., what he called 'pond-dipping' in biology and 'boy scout geometry' in mathematics. Nunn believed, moreover, that even quite young children were very ready to see the practical usefulness of much that is taught. Consequently, he regarded the middle years of schooling as predominantly the utility stage in the course of study. He had most doubts about the propriety of the system stage which he considered to fall rather outside the scope of the secondary school, except perhaps at its highest level. At all events, he attributed the abstractness of traditional teaching to premature preoccupation with the theoretical. Nevertheless, while holding that all branches of the curriculum should be taught as activities rather than as subjects, Nunn was clear that it would be a misfortune if the academic were to disappear from, or be relegated to an inferior position in, school-teaching.

A possible compromise between co-ordination and subordination, as ordinarily understood, is the cyclical system advocated by some writers on education. According to this doctrine no one subject is permanently exalted at the expense of the rest, but intensive periods of study are devoted to certain branches with temporary renunciation of others. In a restricted sense this was the kind of plan adopted by Plato in *The Republic*: during the first stage of education gymnastic alternates with music and later on dialectic with the mathematical sciences. A far more thoroughgoing defence of the system is to be found, however, in the well-known address by A. N. Whitehead on the rhythm of education (1922), reprinted in *The Aims of Education* (1929). Here Whitehead claims that all learning has a natural rhythm in three stages, which he calls romance, precision and generalization, and that accordingly the proper order of studies is to be determined by this rhythm rather than by sheer difficulty or even logical antecedence. The whole course of education, whether we regard it in its entirety or consider it as separate subjects, must in his view follow this rhythm if it is to be effective. At the stage of romance the element of novelty is of supreme importance, and so, initially, knowledge ought not to be dominated by systematic procedure. Too great emphasis on the second stage of the cycle, in which width tends to be sacrificed to exactness, appeared to Whitehead as the main defect in contemporary educational practice. Admittedly the precision stage represents an addition to knowledge, but it necessarily presupposes a prior stage of romance to supply an adequate basis of fact for subsequent analysis. The final stage of generalization is characterized by the classification of ideas and the acquirement of technique, although for Whitehead, as for Nunn, it mainly lies outside the ordinary period of schooling.

The cycle of infancy is comparatively short and is chiefly concerned with the acquisition of speech and reading. This is succeeded at about the age of eight by the cycle of adolescence, during which there is too often either unrhythmic concentration on a single subject or, conversely, undue tolerance of an unrhythmic collection of scraps derived from a multiplicity of subjects. As a happy medium Whitehead advocates a certain measure of concentration and, in especial, avoidance of excessive competition among school subjects at identical stages of their particular cycles. This can best be illustrated in the case of language and science. In language the romantic stage occurs between eight and twelve or thirteen years of age, and from eleven onwards there can well be a gradual concentration on precision. During the precision stage proper the average child should gain command of English, reading fluency in simple French, and an elementary knowledge of Latin. This stage in language coincides, however, with the romantic stage in science, during which the pupils should be permitted to see and experiment for themselves with little in the way of precision. On the other hand, the precision stage in science, coinciding with the transition to the generalization stage in language, is a relatively short one, not exceeding a year in duration. During this period a temporary concentration on science will be essential, in order to enable the pupil to grasp the main principles governing mathematics, mechanics, physics and chemistry. In turn, this will necessarily involve a diminution in language teaching, which at the generalization stage is mainly devoted to literature, with increased attention to its ideas and underlying history. Beyond the age of sixteen a general treatment of development is rendered impracticable, Whitehead maintains, on account of specialization.

Even so, any attempt to implement Whitehead's proposals in the early years of the grammar school must inevitably raise formidable problems of time-table organization. At the same time we should acknowledge that the conventional fixed allocation of teaching periods during the cycle of adolescence may well conduce to rigidity of mind. Out of a 35- or 40-period week, an invariable assignment of (say) 5 or 6 periods to English, French, Latin, mathematics and science, two periods to history, geography, art and craft, and one period to music and religious knowledge, while apparently equitable enough, may in fact have little to commend it apart from administrative convenience. There is no certainty that the teaching of all subjects *pari passu* in this way is necessarily the most efficient or economic arrangement of teaching time. Whitehead's proposals have the merit of envisaging the complete curriculum rather than its constituent elements and, on the whole, they appear to be consistent with the concept of maturation, i.e. intellectual growth of the kind that is relatively independent of external influences. Our aim must be to present knowledge as a coherent whole and not as a miscellaneous collection of unrelated subjects. For this purpose judicious co-ordination is probably the teacher's most effective instrument. At its best it expresses the idea of interconnection between different subjects without artificiality and without dependence. Correlation in the Herbartian sense may be described as a system of cross-references which is most illuminating when a particular school subject is widely illustrated from other subjects.

Our only caution would be that unless a teacher discovers for himself a genuine connection between (say) nature study and poetry, it is futile for him to attempt to illustrate Wordsworth's feelings by merely producing a bunch of daffodils. The specialist teachers of the grammar school in particular appear to experience difficulty in widening their interests without losing essential unity of interest. There may be greater difficulty still in applying co-ordination in the technical school. Here, however, there are no longer the same objections to dependence on a core of leading skills. It may well be that in the case of technical education some form of subordination is to be preferred. We may take, for instance, the vocational interests of the pupils, e.g., science and mathematics, as the integrative force in the curriculum, and utilize that as an organizing principle on which to order the arrangement of their other studies, e.g., English and German. It is for each school to determine in the light of its particular curriculum and the special interests of its teachers how the problem of integration can be most effectively tackled.

Suggestions for Further Reading:

Adams, Sir J., *Exposition and Illustration in Teaching*, Macmillan, 1909.

James, E., *An Essay on the Content of Education*, Harrap, 1949.

Nisbet, S. D., *Purpose in the Curriculum*, U.L.P., 1957.

Nunn, Sir T. P., *Education: Its Data and First Principles*, Arnold, 1945.

Raymont, T., *Modern Education, Its Aims and Methods*, Longmans, 1946.

Rusk, R. R., *The Doctrines of the Great Educators*, Macmillan, 1954.

Whitehead, A. N., *The Aims of Education*, Williams & Norgate, 1932.

CHAPTER IX

THE USE OF TEACHING AIDS

THAT teaching consists of nothing but 'chalk and talk' is a reproach often justifiably levelled against schoolmasters. Yet the attempt has no doubt always been made to simplify, supplement, or clarify arid exposition by means of some form of illustration. Certainly as long ago as 1531 we find Sir Thomas Elyot writing as follows:

And where the lively spirit and that which is called the grace of the thing is perfectly expressed, that thing more persuadeth and stirreth the beholder and sooner instructeth him than the declaration in writing or speaking doth the reader or hearer. Experience we have thereof in learning of geometry, astronomy, and cosmography, called in English the description of the world. In which studies I dare affirm a man shall more profit in one week by figures and charts well and perfectly made than he shall by the only reading or hearing the rules of that science by the space of half a year at the least; wherefore the late writers deserve no small commendation which added to the authors of those sciences apt and proper figures (*The Governour*).

Exactly what figures Elyot had in mind we cannot say, for the first really satisfactory illustrated schoolbook did not appear till 1658, when the *Orbis Pictus* (*World in Pictures*) of J. A. Comenius was published at Nuremberg. This was an introductory textbook to Latin, in which the various items of vocabulary were numbered in the text and illustrated by items correspondingly numbered in a picture at the top of the page. Comenius had thus plainly grasped the fundamental principle of teaching the meaning of words through the sense of sight.

The extent to which teaching aids, aural as well as visual, have come to assist formal instruction in the classroom, is undoubtedly one of the most striking advances in modern education. What we are now in danger of overlooking is that the proper function of illustration is to elucidate, as an adjunct, the matter expounded, not to usurp it altogether. Nor must we forget that unless illustrative material is fully relevant to the matter in hand, the effect may only be to distract the pupil's attention and so, unwittingly, to weaken rather than reinforce the teacher's presentation. In short, we ought always to regard illustration as a means and never as an end in itself. There are, of course, borderline instances. In the case of any given material it may not be easy to draw a hard-and-fast prima facie distinction between its strictly expository and its purely illustrative use. It all depends on the teacher's purpose from one type of lesson to another. He may use a sketch map primarily as a basis for exposition in geography and yet in a French lesson look on it as mainly background material. An anecdote in history may directly convey information, whereas in the poetry period it may be chiefly valuable for illustrating conduct or pointing a moral, e.g. *The Battle of Blenheim,* by Robert Southey. That there may be some merging of functions in this way does not, however, absolve the teacher from being clear in his own mind as to the specific purpose the material is intended to serve in a particular lesson. In the use of teaching aids there are many pitfalls for the unwary, and even the facile assumption that judicious use is wholly beneficial in its effects on the pupil is by no means certain. It is all too easy for an attractive illustration so to monopolize his interest as to exclude concentration on the actual topic, or at all events to divert his attention from the principle that the teacher is attempting to expound.

We do well to remember that there is a subtle variation from one subject to another in the extent to which illustrative methods are fully appropriate. Due care is always desirable, but it may be that slapdash techniques do no great harm in giving a rough-and-ready notion of a coracle or an isthmus. In religious instruction, on the other hand, the slightest inadequacy of representation, by transforming reverence into ridicule, can mar the whole effect of the lesson. It is a common shortcoming of 'home-made' pictorial illustrations that they may fail to maintain a proper proportion between the object represented and the representation itself. The educational consequences of such misrepresentations are not necessarily always serious, but since the human figure is often the chief victim it is as well to guard against possible misconceptions to which they may give rise in children's minds. In a slightly different way this weakness is also characteristic of posters, which though primarily designed for commercial purposes are often put to educational use in the classroom. In these the scale is sometimes deliberately distorted or the colour artificially exaggerated to draw attention to a particular feature of the whole. Again, other pictorial illustrations are apt to overlook the psychological factor known as empathy, whereby the on-looker tends to project himself into the situation represented. Investigations into the physiological and glandular changes caused by both visual and auditory representations of tragic events on child audiences clearly indicate that unconscious feelings of strain and distress are often aroused. We may not always be able to avoid this, but at least in the case of young children particular illustrations liable to give rise to anxiety feelings, such as Atlas supporting the globe on his shoulders or Daniel in the lions' den, can be used with special caution.

The abuse of illustrations by the teacher is, however, a more serious drawback than any defects in the illustrations themselves. Here, perhaps, the chief offence is what

Rousseau calls substituting the symbol for the thing signi-
fied, when this procedure is not absolutely essential. In
other words, it is generally inadvisable to use illustrations if
the objects which they represent can be directly experienced,
even at some inconvenience. The nature study lesson, for
example, will almost certainly be far more effectively illustrated by real leaves gathered by the pupils themselves than
by the clearest representations in manuals of botany.
Another objection to the ill-considered use of illustrations
is the constricting effect they may have in the aesthetic
field on the free activity of imagination. A child's full appreciation of poetry, for instance, may very well be hindered
rather than facilitated by the teacher who presents too concrete a picture of the scene evoked by the poet's words.
Finally, there is always the danger that ill-judged illustrations may actually complicate, instead of simplifying, the
material expounded. Where they fail to come within the
scope of the pupil's experience, this is inevitable. As Alfred
Binet's well-known investigations into children's interpreta-
tions of pictures amply demonstrate, the requisite standard
of reference is by no means easy to determine. It seems that
prior to the age of thirteen children find it far from simple
to relate the individual items in a picture with the central
motif of the whole. No doubt with the gradual extension of
the pupil's experience the standard of reference may be expected to achieve a greater degree of sophistication. But all
the indications are that an indiscriminate use of illustrations
is educationally far less sound than is sometimes supposed.

It is not intended that these cautionary remarks should in
any way depreciate the very real importance of teaching
aids for the effective presentation of subject-matter. One
has merely to examine the clumsy woodcuts of the *Orbis
Pictus* to appreciate what a wealth of material the teacher
of today has at his disposal as compared with his predecessor of three hundred years ago. Nor is it our purpose
to consider in detail either the various kinds of aids or their

specific application to particular branches of instruction. All that can be attempted here is some consideration of the general principles governing their use in the classroom. In speaking of illustration we have had in mind chiefly aids which appeal to the sense of sight, i.e. visual aids, but we should not overlook the other broad category of those which appeal to the sense of hearing, namely, aural aids. Of the two, certainly, it is generally agreed that visual aids have on the whole a greater range of possibilities. The experience which they offer may be at first hand, in the form of visits to works or places of interest or else direct contact with actual objects, such as raw materials, which illustrate manufacturing processes; or it may be rather more vicarious in the form of concrete representations of such objects, e.g., globes, models or miniatures, or else graphic representations of them ranging in complexity from simple diagrams to elaborate mechanical devices. Aural aids, on the other hand, tend to be more definitely vicarious in nature, and they are seldom uncomplicated by a verbal factor. Probably only music and 'sound effects' on radio make a straightforward appeal to the sensory mode of hearing. In the case of others, it is difficult to disentangle the linguistic element, and it is perhaps more accurate to refer to these under the general head of verbal illustration. The fact that deaf children are far more handicapped educationally than blind children should serve as a warning not to overvalue visual at the expense of verbal illustration. For no amount of visual aids will afford deaf children the relative ease in the use of verbal symbols enjoyed by blind children, who are inevitably very largely dependent on aural media of instruction.

Visual aids may be grouped in three main classes of *realia* (i.e. the 'direct' experience mentioned above), pictorial representations, and optical aids. So great indeed is the range of the latter that the term visual aids is now often virtually confined to them alone. Projection pictures with various combinations of colour, movement and sound, in the form of slides, film-strips and films, nowadays offer the teacher a rich variety of media for illustrating his subject-matter in the way that best suits his convenience. Nevertheless, there is still ample room for less sophisticated forms of pictorial aid in the shape of posters, photographs, pictures and even simple graphs. In these days of technical progress the commonplace blackboard still retains pride of place as the most useful single visual aid in the classroom. The individual teacher's own ability to sketch and develop a diagram before the pupils' eyes will always remain one of the most effective methods of graphic representation, and it is a matter for deep regret that blackboard sketchwork involves a degree of skill not given to every teacher. If we disregard the occasional use of musical instruments (e.g., for teaching songs in modern languages), the chief technical aural aids employed in the classroom are the radio, the gramophone (or record-player), and the tape recorder. However, in much the same way that diagrammatic ability is important visually, sheer verbal skill in the use of speech must still be reckoned one of the most valuable assets in a teacher's repertory.

Just how useful direct comparison of the relative effectiveness of visual as against verbal illustration may be is a problematic question. In view of the predominantly concrete nature of children's thinking, preference should no doubt generally be given to the former, where a choice is possible. For the majority of children, at least, it seems well established that object or pictorial illustrations have superior appeal to purely verbal ones; at the adolescent or adult stage, when thinking becomes more abstract, we can expect verbal illustration to gain in effectiveness. Even here, however, the inherent attraction of the visual over the verbal is symbolized by the growing supremacy of television over sound radio in the competition for mass audiences. We must recognize, of course, that television, like the sound film, constitutes a very powerful combination of both visual and verbal illustration which renders comparison with more limited media somewhat inequitable. In their respective developments the one represents the addition of sound to the visual and the other that of the visual to sound. Were it possible to disregard irrelevant factors of cost and convenience, the ultimate triumph of one or other might even have a lesson for the educationist. Both are, however, primarily media of entertainment, and in educational matters it is always advisable to preserve a clear distinction between what is intended to entertain and what to instruct. We may very well find that the kind of thing that superficially makes most appeal is not in the event educationally most effective. If we must make comparisons between visual and aural, it is probably more satisfactory to compare the effectiveness of (say) silent films as against broadcast lessons on sound radio.

Admittedly, apart from the availability of equipment and material, there is probably no good reason for not making the fullest use of technical advances in combining visual with aural. Here, however, we may quote the dictum of the mediaeval philosopher William of Occam that essences are not to be multiplied beyond necessity. This aphorism is known as 'Occam's razor', and it is probably a sound principle in the application of teaching aids. In classifying visual methods there is an unfortunate tendency to grade various forms on the principle that the more sensory modes they appeal to, the more valuable they must necessarily be. On this assumption actual objects appealing to the tactile and kinaesthetic senses, as well as to vision, will be more highly esteemed than mere pictorial representations. Even in the purely visual field stereoscopic pictures in colour, giving a greater illusion of reality, will be preferred to simple monochrome reproductions in two dimensions. Up to a point this is all very well, but it can be carried too far. In education we are not concerned with mass appeal, and when considered in relation to the individual learning of ordinary children, this is a very questionable assumption. A well-known Scottish educationist of the nineteenth century, S. S. Laurie, used to urge: 'Present to sense, present to all the senses.' This may be true, but we are really only justified in multiplying modes of sensory presentation if we have clear evidence of marked differences of endowment from one child to another in respect of predominant imagery. Investigations into children's imagery, however, suggest no such thing. The majority are strong visualizers and, beyond that, the imagery with which their minds are stored is extraordinarily mixed. We may conclude, accordingly, that on the basis of individual differences among pupils there is no need to go to great lengths in providing diversity of sensory presentation. It is far from certain that in general such provision facilitates or reinforces apprehension in the class as a whole, and we cannot be sure that in individual cases simultaneous appeal to various sense modalities may not even have an inhibitory effect on learning.

We may concede, however, that in the past there has been unwarranted neglect in educational practice of what is known as the kinaesthetic sense. This is the sense modality by means of which impressions of movement or muscular effort are built up. Here the implication is that where actual objects are available for illustrative purposes, there is much to be gained by allowing them to be handled, as well as simply looked at, by the pupils. Apart from this, there seems little reason to believe that, by presenting the object or representation to various sense modalities, the teacher would enable some to apprehend and retain it who might otherwise fail to do so. Children's minds are highly adaptable and the mode of presentation does not appear necessarily to determine the mode of retention. Presentation through one mode may readily be translated into a quite different sensory mode for purposes of retention. Smoothness, for instance, is essentially a tactile phenomenon, but we soon come to visualize in the mind's eye as smooth particular objects, such as a plane. Where appeal can be made to an individual's predominant imagery, it is only prudent that we should do our best to meet his needs. But where considerations of time, expense or accessibility restrict variety of presentation, the teacher can usually accept such limitations without undue misgiving. Certainly all the evidence goes to show that little is to be gained in the retention of subject-matter by speciously multiplying the modes employed in apprehending it.

To Rousseau's 'general rule' about the undesirability of substituting the symbol for the thing itself, there are certain particular exceptions that should be mentioned. Some objects, even though available, may not be altogether suitable for introduction into the classroom. A lesson on the structure of the eye, for instance, may be more appropriately taught from a model than from an actual specimen. In other cases, with objects of a certain complexity, such as the functioning of a motor engine or a 16-mm. film projector, a sectional diagram, by virtue of its greater simplicity, may be found in practice more useful for illustrative purposes. In general, nevertheless, it is advisable to be sparing in the use of substitutes and to return afterwards, if at all possible, to the actual object or real situation. If a model loom, for example, is employed in the first instance to teach elementary mechanical principles, the lesson will gain greatly in immediacy for the pupils concerned when a visit is subsequently made to a weaving shed. It is well to remember that the converse is equally true. If actual experiences are to be made the basis for illustrating the practical application of a scientific principle, some measure of theoretical preparation will almost certainly be required for full benefit to be derived from the excursion. The really educational significance of a visit to (say) a waterworks or a brewery will largely depend upon some prior introduction to the principles of hydraulics or fermentation, as the case may be.

Somewhat similar considerations apply to the use of films

for instructional purposes. Though the film is probably the most effective means of visual presentation, it likewise requires both careful preparation and discreet follow-up by the teacher to be of maximum advantage to the pupils. Added to the actual running-time, such complications often raise a practical problem of getting a film lesson to fit into the normal school period. No doubt minor administrative adjustments can usually be made to meet this difficulty, but it is one which undoubtedly makes the frequent use of films in the classroom rather laborious to arrange. From the educational point of view, a more serious objection to films is that the uninterrupted sequence of projected pictures encourages a tendency to passivity among pupils. Nor ought we as teachers to commend unreservedly the implied support of mass instruction inherent in the use of films, in preference to group or individual teaching methods. Nevertheless, educational films have great uses as an aid to learning. They fall roughly into two categories: the so-called 'documentary' films and teaching films proper. Documentaries are useful for filling in background in certain subjects, particularly history, geography and literature. Many of them are, however, sponsored by large industrial enterprises and there is always a certain risk of commercialization in such products. Although, unlike posters, they are specifically designed for educational purposes, they may sometimes serve only to mask covert business interests. Teaching films, on the other hand, actually attempt to deal directly with fresh subject-matter. Perhaps the most famous example is a complete high-school course in physics recorded in the United States by Dr. Harvey White of the University of California in 1957. It consists of 162 half-hour lessons and was produced for use in schools suffering from staffing difficulties in science.

The use of pictures, maps and diagrams for illustrative purposes in most school subjects is so commonplace as to require little comment, except that there is still a tendency to restrict maps to the teaching of geography and diagrams to the teaching of science. As regards pictures it may be said that use of them in the classroom is often much too casual. The proper interpretation of a map would normally be regarded as a matter for some elucidation, but pictures are commonly assumed to be completely self-explanatory. The work of Binet, already referred to, makes it clear enough that this is a fallacy, and that in fact pictures are differently interpreted by children at different stages of development. In matters of scale, particularly, they are often quite wrongly interpreted. Consequently, when a teacher has used pictures to illustrate his subject-matter, he is well advised to cross-examine afterwards to ensure that the meaning he intended has actually been conveyed to the pupils. As a rule, only pictures large enough for exhibition to the class as a whole should be used, for the practice of passing round cuttings from magazines and periodicals merely tends to distract attention. Pictures that are out of date, or wall maps that are over-detailed, are better to be replaced by simple diagrams or selective sketch maps. The latter, when used, need represent only the features required for the immediate purpose, but the same particular care should be taken in preparing them as in constructing graphs or histograms for quantitative illustration in mathematics. In the case of diagrams a quite unpretentious outline may be far more effective than many a more complicated representation. A mediaeval siege, for example, can be more vividly illustrated to the child's imagination by simple 'matchstick' figures storming a square tower than by antiquated pictures of armour, weapons, or Norman architecture. For more exact purposes the so-called Isotype symbols devised by Otto Neurath are a great convenience. This is an artificial term derived from International System of Typographic Picture Education, and it denotes some 2000 standardized symbols representing people, animals, machines, etc., for illustrating data in geography, social

studies and the like. As has been already indicated, it is a
great advantage for the pupils to see sketchwork completed
as the lesson develops. But some teachers, for lack of executive skill or economy of time, may prefer to prepare the
exhibit beforehand on the blackboard, or on a sheet of
drawing-paper for pinning to it.

In the field of aural aids, sound radio is at present the
most highly developed of the mechanical devices, although
the advent of school television now promises fruitful
developments in this medium of instruction. Yet, according
to the comparative report prepared for UNESCO by H. R.
Cassirer, despite the provision of school services by both
BBC and ITA over a period of several years, the impact of
television on education in this country is still very small.
In a highly centralized country like France, a country with
a high illiteracy rate like Italy, or a country with large
sparsely populated areas like the U.S.S.R., far greater use
appears to be made of it. Experiment has been carried
furthest in the U.S.A., where commercial, non-commercial
and closed-circuit television vie with each other in trying
to make good deficiencies in school staffs and equipment.
For demonstration purposes in science or medicine closed-
circuit television seems to offer exceptional opportunities
for a whole class to see clearly the kind of operation they
can at present see singly only under difficult conditions.
Here admittedly the advent of colour is required to complete the process. In this country one or two experiments
have been made to establish communication by this means
between one school and another, but on a very small scale.
As regards official services, some of the obstacles to the
extensive use of school television mentioned are the autonomy of schools to determine their curricula on the one
hand and the examination structure on the other. Although
there are more television sets per head of population in
Great Britain than elsewhere outside the U.S.A., only a
small minority of schools is as yet equipped with them; and

even where they are, television has not managed to establish itself as an indispensable asset. British schoolchildren, being over-sophisticated, tend to compare school television with entertainment rather than with lessons. The result is that, to meet this, producers tend in turn to concentrate on what the Americans call 'enrichment programmes' and to avoid, so far as possible, too much resemblance to schoolwork. Nevertheless, Cassirer sees television as holding great promise for education in the modern age.

Certainly there can be no doubt that school broadcasting has done immensely valuable work in extending the ordinary experience of schoolchildren. Wireless lessons admittedly present the same sort of practical problems as the use of films, for even though they are specifically designed to fit in with the normal length of school period the fixed times of beginning and ending inevitably cut across the ordinary time-table. A more serious educational disadvantage is that the material presented, being relatively uncontrolled by the teacher, may not be directly related to the immediate experience of the particular class of pupils. Like films, wireless lessons require adequate preparation and follow-up work by the teacher, and this can go far towards counter-acting lack of direct relevance. Nevertheless, exclusive dependence on the aural medium emphasizes the speech element and makes it more difficult for the teacher to deliver any comments simultaneously as with (say) a silent film. Variety of voices and accents, far from diversifying the instruction provided, may rather serve to increase the psychological barrier between teacher and taught. This applies also to the gramophone, which is, if anything, even more impersonal than the radio. Like the film-strip in rela-tion to the moving picture, it has, however, the great advan-tage that it can be used for presenting at will good-quality material an unlimited number of times. The gramophone is useful chiefly for developing musical or literary appreciation, or for illustrating linguistic work of various kinds. In the latter, sheer repetition can be of great value to the pupil for helping to absorb into the background memory serviceable secondary material in foreign languages. Unfortunately it is of little assistance in getting him to use this constructively.

Here the tape recorder encourages a more active approach to language work in the classroom. It is not a complicated instrument to put into the hands of the pupils themselves and it is gaining in popularity. For the illustration of good diction or correct intonation, it is of great importance to the learner to hear his own performance recorded. In the teaching of modern languages the international phonetic script can also be a useful adjunct. Rather like Isotype, it represents a scientific attempt to reproduce in graphic form the particular sounds of the foreign tongue. On its own it is unlikely to be very effective, but when taken in conjunction with the gramophone or tape recorder it adds to the purely aural approach a welcome visual element in linguistic work. Drama, recitation and singing are all valuable active forms of verbal illustration which encourage pupil participation. With the youngest children the singing of indigenous folk-songs is no doubt the most spontaneous form of this activity, in which the combination of music with words unites aural and verbal. With older children recitation of national ballads is the next step, though it throws a greater share of the burden on the teacher's shoulders. He must ensure that the meaning of archaic words is fully understood and he will have to declaim the selected passage often enough to fix it in the pupils' minds. Finally, short one-act plays based on some well-known national legend can be attempted. Even without scenery or props, the portrayal in simple everyday speech of life, colour and atmosphere, against a suggestive historical background will sufficiently illuminate the past for the participants.

As with diagrammatic skill, the development of simple verbal facility may be considered too trivial a matter for more than passing mention. Nevertheless, it should be said that oral teaching of any kind that goes beyond plain matter-of-fact statements exemplifies some form of aural illustration, whether explanatory, descriptive or narrative. A telling example that serves to illustrate a rule, or a homely analogy that helps to elucidate some obscure point, is an aid to exposition. Similarly, a striking metaphor or an apt simile adds a descriptive touch to an abstruse or prosaic topic. But probably the most effective form of verbal illustration of this kind is polished narration. Narration includes both a continuous and orderly account of past events in narrative form and any topical anecdote interpolated in the teacher's discourse. The parables in the New Testament are good examples of the use of narration for teaching purposes. Particularly in this oblique form, the story can illustrate a moral principle far more cogently than any straightforward statement, though to do so effectively it must arise naturally out of the lesson itself. To tack a lesson on to a story, on the other hand, is to put the cart before the horse. Where older pupils or adults are concerned, the more pointed and direct the narrative is, the more telling its effects are likely to be. Younger children, however, may sometimes require a certain amount of elaboration and repetition. Nevertheless, however well contrived, any anecdote that savours of a *tour de force* must fail of its effect, for nothing in the world is more certain to fall flat than a story made to order.

Suggestions for Further Reading:

Advisory Council for Education (Scotland), *Visual and Aural Aids*, H.M.S.O., 1950.
Bailey, K. V., *The Listening Schools*, B.B.C., 1957.
Buchanan, A., *The Film in Education*, Phoenix House, 1951.
Crozier, M., *Broadcasting (Sound and Television)*, O.U.P., 1958.
Dale, E., *Audio-visual Methods in Teaching*, Dryden, 1948.
Palmer, R., *School Broadcasting in Britain*, B.B.C., 1947.
Ramshaw, H. G., *Blackboard Work*, O.U.P., 1955.
Sumner, W. L., *Visual Methods in Education*, Blackwell, 1956.
U.N.E.S.C.O., *Television Teaching Today*, H.M.S.O., 1960.

CHAPTER X

EXAMINATION AND ASSESSMENT

In educational practice the proper function of testing is simply the assessment of what has been learned. Nowadays, however, when examinations have come to occupy a disproportionate place in public esteem, they may easily exercise a profound influence on the actual teaching. So much so, indeed, that it is customary to regard examinations as an unmitigated disaster. Yet if possible alternatives, such as the interview, are seriously considered, it is difficult to escape the conclusion that they are a necessary evil in present circumstances. The most natural, as well as the most ancient, mode of assessment is the oral examination, and the written examination as we know it today is a comparative newcomer on the educational scene. The disputations of the mediaeval universities are still recalled in the Cambridge honours examination or 'tripos', so named because of the three-legged stool on which the candidate sat to defend his thesis. In 1748 the university instituted a distinctive mathematical tripos, which became a written examination in 1780. This precedent was rapidly followed at Oxford, where the Public Examinations Statute established the honour school of *Literae Humaniores* (Classical 'Greats') in 1800. Although in practice oral examinations had often been exceedingly casual, it was not that they were necessarily inefficient but simply that with increasing numbers of candidates they had become impracticable. Rather as, more recently, individual intelligence scales have had to make way for the less unwieldy group test, the oral examination was forced to give place to the written test. The sole remaining trace of the mediaeval disputation is the so-called *viva voce*, which may serve simply as a supplement to the written papers or still, in some cases, as a distinctive element in the examination as a whole, e.g., the 'oral' in modern languages or the 'practical' in science.

Once established in the universities, written examinations soon gained a footing in the schools. In 1858 'local' examinations to test school leavers were instituted at both Oxford and Cambridge, and thereafter a multiplicity of external examinations, conducted by professional and other bodies, rapidly came into existence. One of the earliest advocates of public examinations was John Stuart Mill (1806–73), who supported them in his *Essay on Liberty* (1859) as offering a guarantee of competence in particular fields of study and in his *Considerations on Representative Government* (1861) as vastly preferable to the system of patronage for filling vacancies in the civil service. In 1909 the question of examinations in secondary schools was referred by the Board of Education to its Consultative Committee, and the latter in its report two years later urged the co-ordination of such examinations into a clearly defined pattern. No action was taken on this recommendation till 1917, but since then there has been a steadily growing demand to reduce the evil by making one examination serve as many purposes as possible. When the number of candidates exceeds the number of available places, it is obvious that, in the scholastic world as elsewhere, some system of selection becomes inevitable. For this a properly conducted examination is no doubt as objective a basis of assessment as any yet devised. The trouble is that whereas a 'competitive' examination is necessarily more stringent than a 'qualifying' examination designed merely to attest a certain level of academic competence, this distinction tends to be overlooked in practice. Thus a single leaving examination may have the advantage of canalizing a candidate's efforts towards a specific goal. On the other hand, it also has the disadvantage that it may embody diverse purposes which are not really compatible. At best, a reduction in the number of examinations a candidate is required to take must enormously increase the chance effects of the final examination in determining his fate.

Nevertheless, examinations need be looked on as an evil only if their true function is wholly misconceived. When they are seen as an indispensable element in the teaching process, objections to them should largely disappear even in the eyes of the candidates themselves. Regular internal tests, administered as each topic or section of the work is completed, are an excellent corrective to day-to-day fluctuation in the working capacity of individual pupils, particularly in the case of girls. Taken cumulatively, they are certainly preferable to any externally imposed final examination. Such tests, when properly used, may well serve to diagnose weaknesses in a particular pupil's grasp of the subject-matter and thus afford a convenient opportunity for rectifying them. Good methods of testing will doubtless also tend to encourage intelligent methods of teaching and learning. In these days of 'examination conscious' school-children there is little doubt that the particular type of test set will greatly influence the mode of study they adopt. As an example of the more intelligent approach to teaching which modern methods of assessment endeavour to promote, we may cite the various carefully constructed analytic scales of handwriting or composition. By isolating particular items, such as slant and letter formation (or vocabulary and sentence structure), these scales should provide the teacher with more constructive hints for future improvement than the time-honoured, though somewhat nebulous, admonition to do better next time.

So with the pupils. Once given a clear idea of the kind

of assessment they are expected to measure up to, they will readily plan their work accordingly. Appreciation of this fact was one of the strong points in the so-called Dalton Plan, projected at the high school in Dalton, Massachusetts, by Helen Parkhurst in 1922. This was a scheme of educational organization rather than a teaching method as such, and it was designed to apply to the schoolwork of pupils between the ages of eight and eighteen. Although in recent years the plan has rather lost ground, its aim was to solve the problem of differential rates of progress in a class of children. It likewise had the merit of encouraging both self-development and social co-operation among pupils, but what particularly concerns us here was the system of assignments and guide-sheets that governed the allocation of the work. The various subjects studied were divided into monthly assignments and pupils were supplied with guide-sheets outlining the topic to be covered, textbooks to be studied, problems to be tackled, works of reference to be consulted, etc. Individual pupils were left free to proceed as they pleased, provided they contracted to complete all the assignments within the stipulated period. An important feature of the plan was that every assignment in each particular subject contained certain diagnostic checks on the pupil's progress before he was permitted to proceed to the next assignment. It was found that as pupils settled down to the system they became increasingly proficient at regulating their studies so as to complete the assignment within the prescribed period.

Nevertheless, even though continuous internal assessment may render a formal external examination virtually superfluous, experience indicates the undoubted value of a second opinion for supplying a properly objective estimate of attainment. In an external examination the distinctive functions of teaching and examining are perforce completely separated, whereas in an internal test they should be intimately connected. In such a case the teachers concerned should not only play an important part in setting questions and assessing answers, but should also have had a hand in drawing up the original schemes of work. Perhaps the soundest system might be a compromise, as a result of which external examiners should act as a check on internal assessments. This is in fact the system usually in force in universities, but it is more difficult to apply in the case of schools. University examiners generally have two main duties in connection with their task, that of screening the proposed questions and that of reading a proportion of the scripts, particularly the doubtful cases. Under the first head, they may amend wording, add or substitute questions of their own, and generally ensure that the paper as a whole fairly represents the syllabus covered in the teaching; under the second, it is their function to ascertain, after internal assessment, that the standard of marking is reasonable.

The efficient setting of question papers calls for a high degree of skill and experience on the part of examiners. What is not always fully appreciated is that objectivity in the selection of questions is quite as important as any elaborately objective scheme of marking. If, for instance, a majority of questions set should relate to a restricted number of topics covered, the validity of the whole examination might be seriously affected. It may happen, for example, that only three questions are set on (say) ten topics in the syllabus. In this event it would clearly be possible for a lucky student who had concentrated on these to be unduly favoured at the expense of his more industrious colleague who had conscientiously mastered the other seven. Only in very special instances, such as a final examination in medicine or engineering, is it reasonable to expect a candidate to be able to attempt any topic set. Normally the questions should be more or less evenly distributed over the syllabus and every effort be made to counteract the personal predilections of individual examiners. Chance elements can never be eliminated, but examinations constructed in haphazard fashion are specially liable to test powers of prediction just as much as actual knowledge of the subject-matter. If it is clearly impracticable to include in the questions set the whole range covered, a properly random sample of topics dealt with should be made before any decision is taken as to which to exclude.

The expedient generally adopted is, of course, to offer the candidate a choice of questions. This is an obvious convenience and it is usually the fairest way. But should the examination be in any sense regarded as a scientific assessment on which to base direct comparisons of one candidate's performance with that of another, there are certain precautions which ought really to be taken. In a case of this kind it is clearly desirable that alternative questions should be strictly equivalent in standard. The only certain method of achieving this result is to ensure that the mean (average mark) and standard deviation (spread of marks) are approximately the same for each question, although this is an extremely laborious business. So far as marking is concerned, the reliability of an examination is greatly increased if examiners' marks are pooled, but it is not sufficient merely to arrange for different examiners each to mark a given quota of questions and simply aggregate the results. If all do not assess the answers as a whole, the factor of bias is likely to arise in another way. This time it is not so much a question of straightforward prediction as of the candidate's ability to spot questions specifically calculated to score high marks from individual examiners. Admittedly, this will happen only if the examiner's identity is known or can be guessed at with fair assurance, but pupils soon get to know their teachers' foibles (e.g., 'old X is dead keen on the innocence of Charles I', or 'Y hates Cromwell's guts', etc.).

It is commonly objected that the time-limit imposed in most examinations puts a premium on fast working. A positive correlation is known to exist between speed and intelligence, but that is no argument for allowing examinations to degenerate into mere tests of rate of writing. Accordingly, there should always be a generous time allowance in any qualifying examination. Again, much greater care might often be taken to arrange questions in approximate order of difficulty. Even where no prescribed order of answering is laid down, there is inevitably a strong tendency for candidates to attack questions seriatim. Thus a tricky question encountered early on may waste a disproportionate amount of time. In some examinations, indeed, particularly intelligence scales, a direct function of the question order is to assist in determining the proportion of passes and fails in the test as a whole. In other words, the gradation in difficulty in such cases is explicitly intended to eliminate the weaker candidates. Finally, as examinations are at present constituted, there can be no doubt that undue stress is laid on mere reproductive facility. As a result, the candidate with a poor memory for detail is very often unfairly penalized. It is not easy to rectify this anomaly under existing conditions, but one possibility is to allow consultation of basic works of reference, like dictionaries and encyclopaedias, in the examination hall itself. There is no particular correlation between memory and intelligence, and this is commonly done in many continental countries.

Most of the more objectionable features of traditional examinations would no doubt be mitigated if certain elementary measures were strictly observed. Some of these have already been hinted at. In the first place, if our object is to discover what is known rather than to show up ignorance of specific details, clearly the examination paper must fairly represent the ground covered by the teaching. In practice this will generally mean a liberal choice of questions, subject to proper safeguards as to comparability of standard. Secondly, if we wish to avoid putting a premium on the so-called 'smart Alec' mentality, we must ensure plenty of time for answering the paper. Thirdly, if we aim to encourage spontaneity, the questions set will concentrate on the important aspects of the topics selected rather than on abstruse points. It is a doubtful recommendation to know more and more about less and less. Fourthly, to avoid exalting pure memory, we must endeavour to test a grasp of principles rather than sheer reproduction of facts. This is not, however, always practicable in the case of younger pupils. Fifthly, no examiner who seeks to encourage the candidate who genuinely knows his subject, will countenance questions of an ambiguous or disconcerting kind. It has even been facetiously suggested that Shakespeare himself might be puzzled by some of the questions on his own plays now set in English literature papers! Finally, if we wish to minimize the element of chance inseparable from all examinations, teachers' estimates of candidates' probable success should always be taken into account. Such estimates, certainly, are not very helpful unless they can be properly scaled against some objective criterion, but where this is at all feasible it ought to be done.

Another matter which calls for some attention is standardization of the language used in setting examination questions. The position here is often far from satisfactory, although examination questions in particular should demonstrate all the clarity and precision one would like to see characteristic of good oral questioning in the classroom. Yet candidates are required, apparently more or less indiscriminately, to 'discuss', 'examine', 'comment on', 'explain', or 'assess' this or that problem, with little or no indication of the precise distinction (if any) between one instruction and another. Again, examiners are partial to the somewhat dubious device of using deceptively simple circumlocutions that appear to expect quite summary answers when in fact detailed treatment is really looked for. 'Very little' may be the logical answer to 'what light does a shed on b?', or 'not much' to 'how far has x influenced y?'; but it is unlikely that concise answers like these would commend themselves to an examiner. A delegate to the Peace Conference in 1919, when asked to comment on the significance of the Treaty of Versailles, likened it to 'the peace of God, which passeth all understanding'. This is exactly the sort of inconsequential answer that examination questions sometimes seem to invite, yet any candidate who ventured a quip of this kind, however apt, would no doubt render himself liable to proceedings for contempt of schools!

Up till now the traditional so-called essay-type question has been assumed as the norm for purposes of discussion. It must be admitted, however, that the difficulty of objective marking constitutes a serious objection to the exclusive use of such questions in examination papers. A great deal of evidence has been collected to show how hopelessly inconsistent may be the results of purely impressionistic marking. The inherent defect of the essay-type question is, of course, that it attempts to test simultaneously too many heterogenous factors, the relative importance of which has never been precisely determined. It may be a test of, for instance, handwriting ('marks will be deducted for illegibility'), spelling, composition, even originality, rather than of a strict knowledge of the subject of examination. To a certain extent improvements in examination technique can be devised to offset lack of objectivity, but they are unlikely to be more than partially effective. For example, examiners may be instructed to mark strictly on facts or ideas only, and even to list these for checking by the candidates when the scripts are given back. Again, the so-called 'halo effect' that the personality of the examinee may have in colouring the examiner's judgment, can be counteracted by allotting to the candidates, for purposes of identification, numbers instead of their ordinary names. But the only fully effective method of eliminating irrelevant considerations, such as handwriting, composition and the like, is to employ the alternative of the so-called 'new type' test.

The objective or new type test, popular in the United

States, consists of a series of short questions directly relevant to the material to be examined. With these the candidate is clearly aware of what is required of him and has no excuse for omitting anything on the score of inadvertence or forgetfulness. The simplest tests of this kind merely involve 'recognition', and the answers expected are either of the 'yesno' variety, e.g., Lyons is the capital of France . . . yes, no, or else of the 'multiple choice' kind, e.g., Brussels is the capital of . . . France, Belgium, Spain. In either case all the candidate has to do is to underline the appropriate response from among two or more alternatives. It may be remarked in passing that on pedagogic grounds there are certain objections to the 'yes-no' type of answer as tending to suggest wrong information to the pupil's mind. Both types of answer are also liable to encourage random guessing, but they have been found to be fairly effective with young children. Such tests are scarcely searching enough, however, beyond the 11 + stage, and attempts have been made to stiffen them. One device used for this purpose is that of 'matching' (say) a number of historical events from a given period against their appropriate dates. In such a case, to avoid pure elimination, it is necessary to include a somewhat greater number of possibilities than are actually required, e.g.: Bill of Rights; Execution of Charles I; Union of the Parliaments; Authorized Version of the Bible; Union of the Crowns; The Restoration; 1603, 1611, 1625, 1649, 1660, 1689, 1700, 1707. There have also been efforts to make new type tests approximate more closely to the traditional examination involving 'recall', though without the disadvantages inherent in lengthy essay-type answers. In this case the answers expected are generally of the 'completion' type in short self-explanatory statements, e.g., one volt of electricity maintains a current of one —— through a resistance of one ——. Here the candidate has to supply 'amp' and 'ohm' by recall.

It is generally urged against new type examinations that

they fail to test constructive thinking about the basic data, but it may be conceded that the more ingenious items in them, at least, do involve some reasoning. A more weighty objection to the large-scale use of this kind of test is the enormous practical difficulty of preparing suitable questions. Clearly, if new type tests are to claim with justification any greater reliability than traditional examinations, they must in the first instance be more carefully constructed. This is a highly technical matter and only the barest outline of the necessary procedure can be given here. First of all, it is well to ascertain as exactly as possible the various aims held in teaching the subject-matter to be tested. This can be done by both circularizing the schools and consulting the principal textbooks in use. When a selection has been made of those purposes which appear to be most widely accepted, the next task is to list the different aims in order of merit, with a view to determining the relative weight to be attached to them in the final form of the examination. On the basis of this, the preparation of suitable test items having an appropriate bearing on the hierarchy of accepted values can now go forward. Before being administered, however, the resulting trial form of the test should be subjected to expert criticism, and it should contain at least half as many items again as are likely to be required in the final version.

The trial version of the test may now be administered to several groups of pupils for the purpose of making a statistical analysis of the constituent items, in terms both of actual difficulty and of validity as measured by a suitable criterion. Depending on the particular material of the examination, as a rough indication of difficulty we may expect (say) five short items to be correctly completed on average for every two minutes of examination time. The determination of what constitutes a valid criterion, on the other hand, is not always such a simple business. If it is merely a case of gauging attainment, the matter is quite straightforward. The trouble arises when, as so often happens with present-day examinations, the prediction of future scholastic success is a more important consideration than actual academic achievement. Here we are faced with an awkward dilemma, for we may be less concerned with certifying the attainment of a specific standard of knowledge than with attempting to foretell a candidate's probable performance at a future stage in his educational career. The most obvious example of this is the 11 + examination, in which a pupil's present achievement in English, arithmetic and a verbal reasoning test largely determines his suitability in the future for learning foreign languages and science. The intention of such an examination is therefore almost purely predictive, and that of many so-called 'school-leaving' examinations is often not very different. Thus a candidate's performance in the General Certificate of Education may decide his fitness for entering a university (or a technical college) to study medicine (or engineering) without much regard being had, at least in the first instance, to the particular subjects included in his previous course of study. In such circumstances the criterion of validity clearly cannot be some rather vaguely defined standard of knowledge in this or that special field; only high correlation with actual performance, as demonstrated by a careful follow-up of sample groups, will meet the case.

Questions of criterion thus arise even in connection with traditional examinations, and specific measures are sometimes taken to resolve the dilemma so far as may be. The inclusion of the intelligence test in the 11 + examination is an honest attempt to improve its predictability of future achievement. The provision of papers at three levels in the General Certificate of Education is a well-intentioned endeavour to make a leaving examination also serve the purpose of indicating future promise. The ordinary level may be said to represent a reasonable standard of attainment for a 16-year-old pupil in a secondary school. The advanced level is used to prognosticate general fitness to profit from higher education. The special level is designed to determine merit of a sufficiently high order to justify the award of financial assistance for this purpose. In the case of new type tests, the predominant failing is the tendency to elaborate the statistical groundwork at the expense of the items themselves. This development is to be strongly resisted, for unless the utmost care and ingenuity are devoted to the preparation of these no test can be expected to prove satisfactory. Objective test construction admittedly involves the use of quantitative data, and it may be that on occasion the phraseology of new type test items is slightly artificial. Nevertheless, it is important to remember that it is still essentially a creative process which calls for artistic and imaginative qualities on the part of the author. Otherwise, the test can have no hope of diagnosing capacity for organization or interpretative ability, much less originality, on the part of the candidate. By undue emphasis on factual details it may easily have adverse effects on methods of study as well. Moreover, though objectivity of marking may be safeguarded despite faulty construction, proper objectivity in devising the test items can (as with traditional examinations) be all too readily overlooked.

The final form of the test comprises the items selected as most suitable, on the basis both of the item analysis made on the trial version and of comments received from the experts consulted. For ordinary purposes this may very well suffice. If, however, the test must be standardized, it will further have to be scaled on the performance of a representative sample of candidates, to enable direct comparison to be made with other tests or even with alternative forms of itself, cf. Forms *L* and *M* of the Terman-Merrill revision of the Binet Scale. All that now remains to be done is determination of norms and issue of precise directions for administering the test. Norms indicate the level of achievement to be expected at various ages; e.g., reading comprehension (or mechanical arithmetic) in a child of ten. Precise instructions ensure reasonable consistency in standard of administration from one examiner to another. One of the virtues of the new type test is that scoring is purely objective and mechanical. Another is that the wide sampling involved in the large number of short questions to be answered guarantees a higher reliability than the selective sampling implicit in the small number of topics covered in the usual traditional examination. Nevertheless, it should be pointed out that if the traditional examination may be partly a test of facility in writing, this particular feature of new type tests tends to make them in a sense a test of facility in reading. Some people also feel that the gain in objectivity and reliability does not altogether compensate certain educational losses, such as style and clarity of expression. On the other hand, the beneficial effects that new type tests have had in focusing attention on more scientific marking are undeniable, and it may be argued that, if need be, these special qualities can be separately assessed. From the purely practical point of view the two chief disadvantages of new type tests seem to be the burden of work imposed on teachers in setting them and the amount of reading demanded from candidates, especially young children, in answering them. On the whole, however, they are unlikely to be widely adopted in this country in the foreseeable future.

The distribution of marks in any examination is determined by the specific function of the particular test. If the aim is to select scholarship candidates, discrimination will be required at the top of the scale. Hence the number of difficult questions will be proportionately increased. Conversely, if we are concerned simply with a qualifying examination mainly designed to eliminate failure, discrimination will be required at the bottom of the scale. In that case there will be a consequential increase in the number of easy questions. What we must clearly grasp is that, in view of the so-called 'ceiling effect' imposed on candidates at the top of the scale by examinations of low selectivity, it is difficult for one and the same examination to serve both functions adequately. As a rule, raw scores have little meaning in themselves and in school reports to parents they are much more helpful indices of achievement if expressed in 'percentiles'. This is an expression of performance in terms of a pupil's position relative to others in his class or year-group, for a percentile indicates the percentage of cases falling below itself; e.g., the 75th percentile in any group will be attained or exceeded by only 25 per cent of the candidates. Admittedly this task adds to the teacher's labours, but the method of calculating percentiles is not very complicated and can readily be gleaned from any introductory textbook on educational measurement.

In the assessment of essay-type questions where several examiners are involved, little is achieved if the pooling of views is no better than a consensus of worthless opinions. The best way to avoid this situation is for each examiner to assess independently on an agreed marking scheme. According to investigations reported in *The British Journal of Educational Psychology*, it does not appear to matter greatly whether an analytic or general impression method is used in the marking itself. Stephen Wiseman in 1949 reported high reliability by pooling the marks of a team of four examiners of proved consistency who assessed independently the same batch of essays. Lack of consistency may, however, also characterize different performances of the same examinee, and two years later D. S. Finlayson found an almost equally high reliability with only three examiners who marked two essays by each candidate. Unless independence of assessment is strictly observed, there is a danger that the chief examiner, particularly if he has a dominating personality, will unduly influence the final outcome. Where results are amalgamated, or scores from different subjects combined, the standard deviation (or spread), and not the mean (or average), of the candidates' marks will be the determining factor in the weighting of each constituent element. Thus examiners whose marks are closely clustered round a central point, are likely to carry less weight than those who spread their marks over a wider range.

In conclusion, even if examinations are not entirely the bugbear often imagined, some aspects of them are still in urgent need of investigation by research workers. One problem is the whole question of time allowance, which at least in the case of traditional examinations appears to be generally decided quite arbitrarily. It would be useful to know more exactly what is the optimum length of time for examinations in different subjects or at different ages, or how many questions it is reasonable to expect candidates to attempt in the time at their disposal. Another interesting problem is the extent of the influence of temperament on examination performance, and how far allowance might properly be made for candidates who genuinely fail to do themselves justice on account of 'examination nerves'. A third problem is the matter of validity: how can we ever be sure, even with the most rigorous system of marking, that any examination really fulfils the intentions of the examiners? Is it reasonable to expect a single examination to be both prospective and retrospective in intention; e.g., simultaneously a satisfactory criterion for university selection and a suitable attestation of successful completion of a secondary course? A fourth problem is the possibility of providing alternatives to the written examination and, in particular, the proper place of the interview in assessment today. Less exhaustive than the original oral examination, it approximates rather to the 'overall impression' yielded by the essay type of examination answer, and it is inherently subject to the same lack of reliability. Even in the hands of trained interviewers it was convincingly demonstrated by the International Institute of Examinations Inquiry in 1935 just how inconsistent the interview as a method of assessment could be. In a famous instance, out of sixteen candidates interviewed by two boards of examiners, the two candidates placed first in order by each respective panel were found to be assessed eleventh and thirteenth by the other. Yet many people rightly feel that a live situation should somehow afford candidates a wider opportunity of showing their mettle than the more artificial conditions necessarily imposed by a written examination.

Suggestions for Further Reading:

Ballard, P. B., *The New Examiner*, Hodder & Stoughton, 1923.

Brereton, J. L., *The Case for Examinations*, C.U.P., 1944.

Hartog, Sir P. J., and Rhodes, E. C., *An Examination of Examinations*, Macmillan, 1935.

Hartog, Sir P. J., and Rhodes, E. C., *The Marks of Examiners*, Macmillan, 1936.

Jeffery, G. B., *External Examinations in Secondary Schools*, Harrap, 1958.

Lovell, K., *Educational Psychology and Children*, U.L.P., 1958.

McIntosh, D. M., *et alii*, *The Scaling of Teachers' Marks and Estimates*, Oliver & Boyd, 1949.

Valentine, C. W., *The Reliability of Examinations*, U.L.P., 1932.

Vernon, P. E., *The Measurement of Abilities*, U.L.P., 1940.

CHAPTER XI

THE TRAINING OF CHARACTER

THE main emphasis in education is often directed towards promoting intellectual development, although the training of character has always been regarded as both desirable and possible. For many of the great educators of the past the distinction between intellect and character has been at best somewhat tenuous. Socrates, for example, believed not only that it was impossible to do the good without knowing it, but that it was not possible to know the good and fail to do it. In more modern times Herbart has expressed this more forcefully by asserting that the ignorant man cannot be virtuous and that all action springs from what he calls the 'circle of thought'. He held that the human being is more easily approached from the side of knowledge than from that of moral sentiments and dispositions, and thus if instruction is sufficiently systematic it will inevitably result in right action. Without going so far as to identify the moral so explicitly with the intellectual, other educational writers have discussed at length various measures for strengthening or instilling particular moral qualities in the individual pupil. The difficulty was that until they had at their disposal a reasonably coherent theory of the groundwork of character formation, it is hardly surprising that their efforts were somewhat lacking in precision. Until the present century educational psychologists were mainly concerned with problems of sensation, perception, remembering and reasoning, and it is only quite recently that their attention has been turned to the dynamics of behaviour.

The great landmark in changing the attitude of educationists on this question was the appearance of William McDougall's *An Introduction to Social Psychology* in 1908. In this work McDougall formulated his theory of human instincts, as a result of which emotions came to be regarded as concomitants of instincts rather than of ideas in the Herbartian sense. According to McDougall the human mind has certain innate or inherited tendencies which, for convenience, he called instincts. These are the essential motive power of all thought and action, whether individual or collective, and they serve as the bases from which, under the guidance of the intellectual capacities, character is gradually developed. Such a theory accorded well with the traditional view that the systematic development of the intellect has as a kind of by-product far-reaching disciplinary effects upon character, and it was readily accepted by British educationists. It proved less popular in America and was subjected to considerable criticism. Because of the close association of the word 'instinct' with the more inflexible behaviour of animals and insects, McDougall later agreed to substitute the term 'propensities' as more appropriate to human beings. This concession did not, however, satisfy his critics, who continued to urge powerful objections to the whole instinct theory as applied to the case of man. These objections fell under four main heads: firstly, that some of the so-called innate characteristics appear to be really learned early in life; secondly, that as a result of the findings of anthropologists the basic uniformity of human nature is in any case thrown in doubt; thirdly, that in the course of life new drives, seemingly unrelated to inherited modes of behaviour, are acquired; and fourthly, that the concept of instinct is much too abstract to serve any practical purpose.

No doubt the term instinct, like interest, is to be used in

its educational reference with a certain amount of caution. It would be a mistake to believe, for instance, that these innate or inherited tendencies are in no wise modified by the child's everyday experience long before the age of school attendance. Even in their 'pure' state they cannot be regarded in any sense as discrete entities in the child's make-up lying ready to the educator's hand. Nor is the teacher well advised to envisage his task in terms of attempting to stimulate some instincts and to curb others. It is more profitable to think of these tendencies as extremely elastic characteristics which soon become inseparably intertwined and highly complex in their organization. That is not to say that the teacher ought not to be aware of their existence or learn to recognize them when they manifest themselves. Only experience, however, will really show him in any particular case which impulses may be enlisted to assist his efforts, and which must be checked as obstructive of them. Nevertheless, we may admit that the primitive behaviour patterns inherited by children, except that they are far more readily modified, do have some analogy with the instinctive mechanisms of the animal world. An essential part of McDougall's theory was that as children grew up the emotional elements in these so-called instincts became organized into particular attachments to persons or ideas in a way which integrated emotional life and so rendered behaviour relatively consistent and predictable. Indeed, A. A. Roback defined character as 'an enduring psychophysical disposition to inhibit instinctive impulses in accordance with a regulative principle' (*The Psychology of Character*).

McDougall's original list contained twelve human instincts, five of which were regarded as of less well-defined emotional tendency, although McDougall did not deny that they might none the less have impulses of considerable importance for social life. These were the reproductive, food-seeking, gregarious, acquisitive and constructive instincts.

The seven so-called principal instincts, on the other hand, had associated with them primary emotions that were sufficiently easily recognizable to have definite names in common speech. They were flight (fear), repulsion (disgust), curiosity (wonder), pugnacity (anger), self-abasement (subjection), self-assertion (elation), and the parental instinct (tenderness). To the original twelve McDougall afterwards added the instincts of appeal (distress) and laughter (amusement), and still later four lesser 'propensities', namely, to wander, to seek physical comfort, to rest when exhausted, and to satisfy certain bodily needs which are not purely reflex in nature (e.g., coughing and sneezing). By innate or inherited McDougall did not mean to imply that all these instincts must necessarily be found in full operation in a newly born infant. While the requisite mechanisms are no doubt present from birth, it would be quite reasonable to suppose that a certain degree of maturation (as distinct from learning) might well be required to set them in motion.

Accordingly, it could prove a rewarding if somewhat elusive task for the teacher to try to determine with reasonable assurance at what age in the course of the child's development various instincts emerge or attain their strongest urge. Fortunately for him, one of the earliest to manifest itself is curiosity, which is usually sufficiently highly developed by the age of seven to be utilized for specifically educational purposes. The constructive instinct, again, seems to emerge relatively early and to remain characteristic of the primary school child from the age of eight onwards. On the other hand, the migratory impulse and the pugnacious instinct do not usually reach their peak till about nine or ten, but, if left unchecked, they can easily then lead to truancy and bullying. Somewhat later, about ten or eleven, the acquisitive instinct makes its appearance, and it too may result in delinquency in the form of stealing, unless the passion for collecting things can be turned to account by inculcating respect for property. The onset of puberty is marked by maturation of the reproductive instinct, and development of the gregarious impulse characterizes early adolescence. Finally, the vocational aspirations of later adolescence represent in a generalized way the emergence of the food-seeking instinct, which in the case of primitive man was doubtless originally canalized in hunting activities. Although, therefore, we cannot be certain about the genetic origin of human instincts, we need not allow the differential rate of their emergence in the child, of itself, to invalidate McDougall's theory. The practical importance for the teacher of determining the age at which they appear is not only that he may utilize them to train character but also that, in the form of interests (with which they are closely allied), they may likewise serve to foster intellectual growth.

The other objections to instinct theory can also be more or less satisfactorily disposed of. The fact that different culture patterns may in practice influence manifestations of particular traits, as observed by anthropologists, does not conclusively prove the absence of all tendency to action of a certain kind. In other words, even though a primitive tribe appears to show a complete absence of aggression or dishonesty, this may not really imply that the pugnacious or acquisitive instinct is wholly lacking. The correct inference may simply be that it is overlaid by the particular *mores* of the tribe in question. Similarly, the fact that in the course of life new drives are acquired, of the kind which psychologists call 'functionally autonomous' (i.e. apparently independent of primitive impulses), does not preclude the possibility that they may still, at the unconscious level, derive their psychic energy from instinctive sources. Finally, the purely hypothetical character of instinct need not deter us from acting on the assumption that it has a real existence, any more than the abstract nature of intelligence has stood in the way of empirical attempts to measure human ability for practical purposes. At worst, the various objections to the concept of instinct need only impress on us the necessity for caution in relying too firmly on inborn patterns of behaviour in any scheme of character training.

Human behaviour for McDougall was essentially purposive in nature and he invested it with six distinctive characteristics. In the first place, he saw it as spontaneous rather than mechanistic. Secondly, he considered that it persists independently of the original stimulus. Thirdly, it was persistently varied until change of a kind is effected that is predictable in terms of a general knowledge of human nature. Fourthly, he claimed that it ceases as soon as this change has taken place. Fifthly, he held that it prepares for the resulting situation. Finally, he noted that on subsequent recurrence, under similar conditions, some improvement in execution may be effected. As an indication of the lines on which character training may be attempted, this general analysis of human behaviour alone is of some value. By a particular analysis of successive phases in the operation of specific instincts, however, McDougall makes a still more notable contribution to the possibility of modifying such behaviour. The pattern of instinctive reaction in any situation he described as being that a certain class of objects is apprehended, emotional excitement is aroused and a tendency to action is experienced. These are the cognitive, affective and conative phases of the instinct, and McDougall contended that once the main instinctive reactions of man were determined it would be feasible to set about modifying one or more of these phases. In view of the fact that the affective phase is particularly vital in the training of character, it is perhaps unfortunate that McDougall himself was more hopeful of the possibility of modifying the cognitive and conative phases of instinct. Nevertheless, there are good grounds for believing that some modification even of the affective phase may well be possible, particularly in the case of the group of instincts of less well-defined emotional tendency.

So far as modification of the cognitive phase is concerned, the instinct of curiosity appears to offer the widest scope for the educator's ingenuity. The kind of objects envisaged by McDougall as naturally arousing this instinct seem to be generally of a fairly concrete nature. On the other hand, it is obviously essential in the moral and spiritual sphere to accustom children to react to abstract ideas associated with such objects. Curiosity about religion and other abstractions can be stimulated only at the ideational level, and here the wise use of visual and aural aids can often assist in effecting the transition from concrete to abstract. Undue insistence, however, on always confronting pupils with actual objects or real situations, can easily have the opposite effect of ignoring all possibility of modification. Even if the teacher succeeds, without too great reliance on concrete support, in raising curiosity to the ideational level, there is still a strong likelihood that the ideas implanted in the pupils' minds will largely centre round natural objects. It is improbable, therefore, that simple modification of the instinct of curiosity will be effective beyond the child's natural interests. If ideas not noticeably connected with instincts are also to provide incentives to action, resort must be had to the process of sublimation, whereby impulses are deliberately redirected into activity of greater social value. Sublimation of the instinct of curiosity leads to the growth of acquired interests, and the curiosity which, in popular parlance, killed the cat, may, if properly channelled, produce disinterested researchers into theoretical aspects of knowledge.

As an example of the kind where modification of the affective phase of an instinct is desirable, we may cite the case of flight. According to McDougall, this is one of the major instincts that condition some one kind of emotional excitement whose quality is peculiar or specific to it. In the case of flight, the affective reaction is fear, and if the teacher merely tries to block the tendency to run away, it may simply seek some outlet that will involve continued failure to face up to danger. In such circumstances the wiser course is to endeavour to train pupils not to experience panic in situations of danger. That is in fact what the teacher tries to do in inculcating such precautions as kerb- or fire-drill in school. We may perhaps regard this as a somewhat trivial instance. From this point of view a more fruitful application of McDougall's system is his treatment of blended or fused emotions. These are peculiar to man and they result from the simultaneous excitement of more than one instinct by the same object or situation. When this occurs, the accompanying emotions blend to form new complex emotions, such as gratitude, admiration and awe. Some of these are among the most powerful drives motivating moral conduct, and it is the teacher's business to devise, if he can, appropriate situations in the classroom designed to evoke such reactions in his pupils. In this way qualities like reverence, altruism and the sympathetic approval of good deeds can be developed into permanent elements in character.

A significant feature of McDougall's theory was that, as with other mental characteristics, the degree of strength of instinctive reactions varies considerably from one individual to another. In extreme instances he therefore regarded sublimation of the affective phase of instinct as very necessary, especially in the case of potentially antisocial instincts. In an individual strongly endowed with the instinct of pugnacity or of self-assertion, the slightest cue may arouse violent anger or intense 'positive self-feeling'. The solution here is to dissociate the instinctive reaction from the kind of situation that naturally arouses it and to redirect it, where possible, towards a socially approved objective. With careful treatment a pugnacious lad may thus be turned into a potential social reformer or an unduly self-assertive boy into a budding patriot. With instincts of less well-defined emotional tendency, it is often sufficient to concentrate on the conative phase, or on the affective-conative phases in conjunction. Indiscriminate appropriation of whatever happens to catch the child's fancy is very often the outcome of the acquisitive instinct when unchecked. In this instance we may simply check the conative reaction without necessarily discouraging its accompanying love of ownership, because of the important bearing this can have on business enterprise later on. On the other hand, with the reproductive instinct we may think it desirable that both the affective and conative phases should be modified. In giving sex instruction we should, therefore, seek not merely to check promiscuity but also to refine the accompanying sexual excitement.

Here, admittedly, we encounter a difficulty, of which McDougall was not unaware, namely that some instincts cannot be thought of in terms of reaction to external stimuli alone but must be regarded as partly determined by sensory stimuli from within the organism itself. The reproductive instinct is a case in point. It is aroused either by an external erotic stimulus, such as a member of the opposite sex, or by an internal bodily state of tension—or, it may be, by a combination of the two. The teacher, however, is not concerned with the metabolism of his pupils' endocrine secretions, and so his efforts are perforce confined to the purely external manifestations of the sex impulse. In a good many cases, accordingly, we can expect them to be, at best, only partly successful. McDougall nevertheless maintained that any modifications effected in original responses could be transmitted by the organism in a cumulative way to succeeding generations. This theory, based on McDougall's researches into the training of rats in a submerged maze, is an attractive one for educationists, but in the light of the evidence produced its validity must be considered highly suspect. Even if we might accept the possibility of such an occurrence in an artificial laboratory situation, it could have little relevance for ordinary educational purposes. Real life situations could hardly be expected to reproduce sufficiently constant or similar conditions to prove the value of inherited training of the type envisaged by McDougall. The teacher is well advised, therefore, not to entertain illusions about the progressive perfectibility of man, but to be satisfied if he succeeds in effecting even a slight modification in the instinctive responses of his immediate charges.

The various instincts as postulated by McDougall have still to be differentiated on a scientific basis and we may possibly entertain reservations as to the completeness of the list he proposes. It is, however, difficult to deny the general bearing of his work on the problems of the classroom. Even though a good deal of the routine activity of children can be more or less mechanically conditioned, character training of a more complex kind does appear to require some such explanation as McDougall's account of the operation of instinct. Unless the individual is endowed with some intuitive means of apprehending situations as relevant for the performance of this or that line of action, it would seem futile to devise moral codes to which behaviour must conform. Clearly instinct, which McDougall regards as essentially purposive and guided by intelligence, provides us with a plausible account of the requisite appraisal of, and subsequent response to, problems of a moral kind. McDougall's treatment of the cognitive aspect of instinct ensures the essential *savoir-faire* or insight to respond appropriately to novel situations. His insistence on emotion as the core of instinct supplies the dynamic of the moral will. His conception of the possibility of canalizing instinctual energy in sublimation would account for man's acquiring fresh drives 'overlaid' by experience. Indeed, his whole theory of the formation of sentiments around objects, ideas and people encountered in everyday life, explains the contribution of ordinary experience to personality in terms that correspond closely with the traditional notion of conscience.

What McDougall does, perhaps, overlook is a qualitative difference in human behaviour which is difficult to explain merely in terms of complexity. He appears to regard human

volition of the highest moral order as simply a more complex conjunction of impulses that can be traced right down
the evolutionary scale to the animal world. Dewey freely
acknowledges the biological continuity of human impulses
and instincts with natural energies, but most idealist
educators would prefer to postulate in man a unique moral
capacity which, though it may well combine with the so-
called instinctive tendencies, cannot be generated out of
them. Even when it combines with natural impulses, this
moral power so transmutes them as, in a sense, to regenerate
the tendencies themselves. Certainly it is difficult to envisage
such urges in man as emulation, shame, or sex as part of
a continuum of animal instincts and emotions. Another
respect in which McDougall's hypothesis of instinct fails to
provide the teacher with an entirely satisfactory basis for
action is the reliance placed on mere differential strength of
drive from individual to individual. If, for example, every
case of kleptomania, or of persistent truancy, or of aggres-
sive bullying in pupils is attributable purely to an abnor-
mally strong acquisitive, migratory, or pugnacious instinct
(as the case may be), the teacher is left with very little room
for manœuvre. His only remedy is to endeavour to sublim-
ate the impulse by redirecting its energy into other channels.
This, indeed, he may often do in an attempt to prevent
undesirable traits from developing, but he does well to
recognize that deep-seated symptoms of such a kind are
beyond his scope. Some thieves, truants, or bullies are
morally delinquent in the sense that their actions are trace-
able to specific predisposing causes which require therapeutic treatment by experts in a child-guidance clinic. In
their case no amount of straightforward checking will have
any effect.

It may be wondered why McDougall did not posit a
moral instinct as such in his list of human propensities. In
rejecting this notion he no doubt rightly discerned that
morality in its operation is too pervasive to be related to any

one specific instinct. We are thrown back, therefore, on the traditional assumption that each individual is endowed with an innate sense which enables him to perceive more or less intuitively whether a contemplated action is morally right or wrong. It would be a mistake, however, to conceive this faculty as a moral sense existing in isolation or independently of the intelligence. It is rather a capacity for moral judgment which develops both in the race and the individual, and is extremely sensitive to modification by environment and education. In addition to the instincts, McDougall also lists the general or non-specific tendencies of suggestion, sympathy, imitation and play. A good deal of social cohesion can clearly be accounted for by the first three, and there seems no reason to doubt that skilful exploitation of the play tendency can serve as a useful focus for imposing on natural impulses a pattern of socially acceptable activities. The characteristic approach to character training in British schools has, therefore, been through games, and while such a conception is no doubt sometimes crudely applied it appears to be well grounded in principle. Even so general a tendency as the play impulse assumes in the child a quite different significance from that of its counterpart in the animal world. Mastery of physical skills has a peculiar appeal for the majority of schoolboys. Plato also held that 'gymnastic' had in view the good of the soul as well as the body.

In the early stages a good deal of moral training is undoubtedly transmitted through play, habit and convention, but virtue, unlike the vernacular, is not unwittingly acquired through social intercourse. Morality is not merely a matter of doing; it is far more a product of thought and reflection. Indeed, the highest moral action is directed by enlightened sympathy, and this demands in the later stages of education a definite course of moral instruction. The regulative principle, referred to by Roback in his definition of character, is constituted by what may be called the moral ideal, which requires to be realized in the pupil's actions very much as his other studies have to be assimilated by his intellect. Traditionally, the moral ideal comprises some rather vague system of virtues, such as those outlined by David in Psalm 15 or by St. Paul in the fifth chapter of Galatians. For Plato the moral ideal, as sketched in *The Republic*, is to be justice, or uprightness in the individual life allied to righteousness in social life. This is seen to be compounded of temperance or self-control, courage, and wisdom, and it is the business of the educator to foster them in the pupil in much the same way as McDougall envisages the growth of sentiments. In contradistinction to the primary emotions, a sentiment is a learned and structured pattern of behaviour, and it is defined as an enduring conative attitude towards some object induced by experience of that object. In his book, *On Education, Especially in Early Childhood*, Bertrand Russell depicts for the educator what he calls a right conception of human excellence. Four characteristics seem to him jointly to form the basis of an ideal character, and these he designates vitality, courage, sensitiveness and intelligence. He considers that this list, though possibly not complete, carries us a good way, and that the building up of character involves chiefly the first three of these qualities. In moral, as in intellectual, education the tendency to exalt one virtue to the exclusion of all others is to be avoided, and to some extent this is guarded against if our moral ideal consists of a system of virtues.

If the moral judgment requires to be developed through a course of instruction, the final questions to be considered are those of treatment and method. Moral instruction differs from intellectual in that the treatment need not be systematic nor the method direct. Indeed, at different stages of moral development there is much to be said for incidental treatment or indirect method, as circumstances may require. Though our knowledge of the growth of moral ideas in the child is far from complete, work done in constructing

intelligence tests has thrown some light on the ages at which
ethical concepts are normally formulated. Thus L. M.
Terman, when making the Stanford revision of the Binet
Scale, noted that in the interpretation of fables children of
nine or ten took the story quite literally and only at fourteen
or fifteen did they fully appreciate the moral behind it.
Rousseau also, while rejecting the use of fables prior to the
age of twelve as liable to mislead, recognized that, in adolescence, when we blame the guilty under cover of a story we
instruct without offending him. 'The time of faults is the
time for fables', as he succinctly puts it. Terman likewise
found a considerable growth in the ability to define abstractions, like pity or revenge, between eleven and thirteen. At
the earlier age definitions tended to be particularized to
a specific context, whereas later they were sufficiently
generalized to indicate an abstract understanding of ethical
concepts.

By incidental treatment is meant the casual consideration
of moral questions as they arise, and by indirect method the
inferring of moral principles from anecdotes or parables.
From what has been said, it will be clear that the indirect
method is unsuitable for young children. Nor is it desirable
that for them the treatment should be too systematic. Hence
in the primary school the most appropriate kind of ethical
instruction is to draw moral lessons from chance incidents
occurring in the classroom; e.g., lying or stealing. With
older children exactly the opposite obtains. The direct
method is less palatable and treatment should be much more
systematic. That is why a prescribed set of lessons such as
a catechism, e.g. Kant's suggested catechism of right conduct explaining how the principles of morality apply to
situations of everyday life, has fallen out of favour. On the
whole, we now tend to prefer a planned course of biography,
drama, or lyric poetry, while leaving the pupils to draw
their own conclusions from the text. The reason for this is
that direct moral instruction, involving the exposition of

moral judgments in a purely generalized form, fails to arouse the required emotional response in pupils. It is only when they are presented with specific examples of human behaviour in a wide variety of situations that sympathy is enlightened and high endeavour is actively kindled in the imagination.

Suggestions for Further Reading:

Hardie, C. D., *Truth and Fallacy in Educational Theory*, C.U.P., 1942.

McDougall, W., *An Introduction to Social Psychology*, Methuen, 1908.

Peel, E. A., *The Psychological Basis of Education*, Oliver & Boyd, 1956.

Peters, R. S., *Authority, Responsibility and Education*, Allen & Unwin, 1959.

Roback, A. A., *The Psychology of Character*, Kegan Paul, 1927.

Russell, B., *On Education, Especially in Early Childhood*, Allen & Unwin, 1926.

Smith, F. V., *The Explanation of Human Behaviour*, Constable, 1951.

CONCLUSION

THE successful teacher, Bacon tells us, is the one who transplants knowledge into the scholar's mind as it grew in his own. While this may not always be the case, it does suggest that there is much to be gained from putting our own minds on a level with those of our pupils and appearing to learn along with them. So long as teaching remains a personal art rather than an exact science, there can be no finality on the question of method. The expository powers of different teachers take different forms, individual differences in learning capacity among pupils require variety of approach, and the heterogeneous nature of school subjects precludes conformity to any one definitive system. Method is a good subordinate but a bad dictator, and, indeed, most subjects will be found to suggest their own rules and expedients to the teacher's common sense if he cares to reflect on them. We may suspect that those who are too ready to favour any particular method, are in fact apt to choose their examples to suit their own convenience. They may even be inclined to advocate the teaching of subjects that are amenable to the kind of procedure they prefer. Since declensions and formulae leave little room for argument, the dogmatic teacher will no doubt proclaim the merits of the classics or of mathematics. The speculative teacher, on the other hand, may prefer history or science as giving the pupil more scope for genuine discovery. The progressive teacher may well consider that dramatics or geography offers the pupil greater possibilities for learning from experience. To some extent it is a question of temperament.

Another factor which has an important bearing on method is the question of pupil organization. What is possible with small numbers of pupils may not be feasible with large classes. John Locke believed that as each child's mind was unique, the only satisfactory arrangement would be a private tutor for every child. Clearly this idea is out of the question in a modern industrial society, but there may still be a place for individual methods in the school today. In the early stages acquisition of skill in both reading and writing is almost wholly a question of individual teaching. When mastery of fundamental skills has been achieved, opportunities can be found for individual work in which pupils can utilize silent reading periods to discover for themselves a fair amount of preliminary material. More important still, towards the end of school life, it becomes increasingly desirable to foster the habit of private study by getting the pupils to supplement the information in their textbooks through learning to use commoner works of reference. The important point to be grasped here is that many teachers conceive it their duty to be always teaching, when in fact the spirit of inquiry and research might often be better served by leaving a far greater share of the work to the pupils themselves. The Montessori apparatus in the case of younger children and the Dalton Plan with older pupils implicitly recognize this fact.

Method really only comes into the picture, however, when the teacher is concerned with collective instruction. Here the traditional unit of organization is the class; and, provided it is not allowed to degenerate into drill, ordinary class teaching can still be justified on grounds of suitability or of administrative convenience. The modern practice of streaming has certainly contributed, in larger schools at least, to making classes more homogeneous for teaching purposes. The further streaming of pupils into sets for particular subjects in the secondary school is another step in the same direction. The kind of subjects that particularly lend themselves to collective treatment has aready been indicated. The appreciative subjects, such as literature, history, and aesthetics, make a natural appeal to the nascent gregarious instinct of adolescence, but communal activities like singing and dancing are also essentially collective in nature. Under the head of administrative convenience probably the most important use of class teaching is demonstration of some new step in mathematics or rule in a foreign language. A class lesson can also be of value for the revision and integration of knowledge acquired incidentally in the course of informal activities. Again, class teaching may be useful as a means of introducing unusual objects or material, e.g. a photostat manuscript in a history class or dissection of a sheep's heart in a biology lesson. Class teaching has more intangible uses in diagnosing, elucidating and amplifying the various errors, difficulties and achievements of pupils. General misconceptions may be revealed by the give-and-take of oral questioning, common difficulties may be noted in written work by the teacher in the course of going round the classroom, and deficiencies of individual work can be made good from his superior stock of knowledge. For all these reasons collective instruction is unlikely to be entirely superseded.

A possible compromise between individual and class instruction is group activity, in which a class is split up into half a dozen small groups for special purposes. This is sometimes done on an ability or achievement basis to facilitate progress in reading or arithmetic; but, like class teaching, it may have an administrative justification. Such is particularly the case when expensive apparatus and equipment is involved. The cost of providing each individual pupil with a set may be prohibitive, yet if the teacher alone handles the materials valuable opportunities for learning may well be lost. The obvious solution is to purchase sufficient equipment to cater for a few groups, so that the benefits of direct contact can be extended to the maximum number of individual pupils. Progressive educationists, however, claim that the social value derived from co-opera- tive work is a far sounder justification for grouping in a class of pupils. They generally have some form of the Project Method in mind, and they tend to regard traditional class teaching not only as inefficient but as lacking in respect for the child's individuality. For them the only acceptable basis for group work is community of interest in some aspect of a common problem which fosters respect for others, as well as developing in the individual himself useful habits and acquirements. Such people are apt to overlook the need for competition in addition to co-operation, but group work in the form of teams can often stimulate interest without encouraging the intense rivalry sometimes fostered by old- fashioned collective teaching.

Method in education is to be regarded as a system of valid principles which, when liberally conceived, will not only be of service to the teacher but will preserve him from developing into a pedant. It is no substitute for knowledge, and unless it is brought to bear on genuine scholarship it is liable to degenerate into mere rule of thumb. The purpose of method is, therefore, to apply a sufficiency of knowledge in the most effective way; it is in no sense a mechanical technique which tends to regard subject-matter as material for the exercise of pedagogic skill. Nor is method any substitute for first-hand experience, although its study can give valuable insight into the workings of young minds. If method is overdone, it tends to conduce to dogmatism, but in some circumstances it can have the effect of undermining confidence. The grammar school master who teaches from a full knowledge of his subject without having ever examined his procedure in the critical light of method may be unaware of any problem. The diligent student of method, on the other hand, may be constantly inhibited through fear of going wrong. Though the principles of method may be communicated as counsels of perfection, it is only in vigorous action that they can be mastered. The experienced teacher who learns to make his study part of himself, has at his disposal a pedagogic capital on which he may draw almost unconsciously. This is our own aim in studying method, and if it is lacking in scientific rigour we should remember Rousseau's paradox that the scientific atmosphere destroys science. In teaching, no less than in preaching, the letter killeth but the spirit giveth light.

GLOSSARY OF TECHNICAL TERMS

Anschauung (Pestalozzi): lit. 'intuition", or the process whereby the child's direct experience of objects is transformed in his mind first into clear images and subsequently into definite ideas.

apperception (Herbart): the mental process as a result of which new perceptions and experiences tend to be conditioned by existing mental content. Relevant previous experiences constitute an appropriate frame of reference, or system of ideas, called an 'apperception mass'.

cognitive, affective, conative: refer to the intellectual, emotional and purposive aspects of mental life.

concentration (Herbartian): the focusing of subordinate studies round a core subject as a means of integrating knowledge in the pupil's mind.

correlation (Herbartian): the interrelating of co-ordinate subjects by means of cross-references to common aspects and processes with a view to presenting knowledge as a coherent whole.

heurism (Armstrong): the principle in education whereby the pupil is set to find out things for himself, particularly in connection with scientific discovery.

ideational: refers to the level of mental life at which the pupil is capable of dealing with abstractions and is no longer dependent on the presence of concrete objects.

objective (new type) tests: examinations composed of a large number of short items in contradistinction to the traditional type that require comprehensive answers on a small number of topics.

sense modality: any of the sensory modes by which external objects are perceived, e.g. vision, hearing, touch.

sublimation (McDougall): a term borrowed from Freud to describe the redirection of instinctive energy into socially approved channels.

syncretic (Comenius): refers to the method of attempting to reconcile mental phenomena with the organic processes of nature.

INDEX